PENTECOSTAL EXPLORATIONS FOR HOLINESS TODAY

WORDS FROM WESLEY

PENTECOSTAL EXPLORATIONS FOR HOLINESS TODAY

WORDS FROM WESLEY

RANDY HOWARD AND TONY RICHIE

Cherohala Press
Cleveland, Tennessee

Pentecostal Explorations for Holiness Today
Words from Wesley

Published by Cherohala Press, an imprint of CPT Press
900 Walker ST NE
Cleveland, TN 37311
USA
email: cptpress@pentecostaltheology.org
website: www.cptpress.com

Library of Congress Control Number: 2017933241

ISBN-10: 1935931636
ISBN-13: 9781935931638

CONTENTS

CONTENTS

INTRODUCTION

A Methodist: If you walk by this rule, continually endeavoring to know and love and resemble and obey the great God and Father of our Lord and Savior, Jesus Christ, as the God of love and of pardoning mercy; if from this principle of loving, obedient faith, you carefully abstain from all evil, and labor as you have opportunity, to do good to all men, friends and enemies; if lastly you unite together to encourage and help each other in working out your salvation, and for that end watch over one another in love – you are they whom I mean to call Methodists.[1]

– John Wesley

The assertion of this volume is that the experience of sanctification which has been prominently espoused by many groups for approximately 200 years has all but disappeared. With even more certainty, it can be said that sanctification as a second work of grace has disappeared. Both writers speak as third-generation ministers in the Holiness-Pentecostal tradition where sanctification as a second blessing has been securely anchored for several generations. Yet when this theme is addressed among ministers and leaders, as well as at the only Holiness-Pentecostal seminary in the nation, the Pentecostal Theological Seminary, the assertion has never been challenged that sanctification has declined so far that it is totally off the radar. In addition, sanctification as a process forming lives and purifying lives in holiness can only rarely be heard in sermons. It is as if the word has been erased from the vocabulary of preachers and teachers in the Christian world. A brief search of the internet will

---

[1] Paul Wesley Chilcote, *Recapturing the Wesleys' Vision: An Introduction to the Faith of John and Charles Wesley* (Downers Grove, IL: IVP Academic, 2003), p. 102.

reveal numerous articles and discussions about the general decline in sanctification and holiness.[2]

In a 2003 study on holiness by the Barna Group, the 'results portray a body of Christians who attend church and read the Bible, but do not understand the concept or significance of holiness, do not personally desire to be holy, and therefore do little, if anything to pursue it'.[3] While we address this topic (holiness) from our particular perspective of the Holiness-Pentecostal tradition, it is relevant for the broader Christian tradition as well.[4] Tyler Braun is a 'twenty-something' Christian writer who said the following about his generation:

> As the next generation of young Christians (including myself) continues to root themselves well within culture, we've lost the marks that allow Christ to be seen by a world that denies him. We've lost holiness. Young believers have pursued life experience at the expense of innocence as we've given up on caring about the sin in our own lives.[5]

And young cultural critic Brett McCracken joins the mounting tide of voices that lament, 'there is no difference between believers and non-believers in our land today'.[6] Yes, we have lost holiness.

---

[2] Keith Drury, 'The Holiness Movement is Dead, Counterpoint Dialogue' online, accessed May 15, 2015, http://www.fwponline.cc/v24i1/review%20two. html.

[3] Barna Group, 'The Concept of Holiness Baffles Most Americans', online article, accessed May 15, 2015, https://www.barna.org/barna-update/5-barna-update/162-the-concept-of-holiness-baffles-most-americans/.

[4] The historical and theological interconnectedness of the Wesleyan-Holiness-Pentecostal traditions is tight. See Tony Richie, 'Pentecostalism's Wesleyan Roots and Fruits', *Seedbed* (March 14, 2014), http://www.seedbed. com/pentecostalisms-wesleyan-roots-fruit.html.

[5] Tyler Braun, 'What We Have Lost Does Not Outweigh What We Have Gained', as quoted in Drew Dyck, *Yawning at Tigers: You Can't Tame God So Stop Trying* (Nashville: Nelson Publishers, 2014), p. 45. Braun's article can be found online at http://manofdepravity.com/2012/09/loss-gain/, Man of Depravity blog, accessed May 15, 2015. Braun also has written – *Why Holiness Matters* (Chicago: Moody Publishers, 2012).

[6] Brett McCracken, 'Have Christians Lost Their Sense of Difference?' as quoted in Dyck, *Yawning at Tigers*, p. 45. McCracken's article can be found at http://mereorthodoxy.com/have-christians-lost-their-sense-of-difference/Mere Orthodoxy online, accessed May 15, 2015.

The word 'exploration' is used in the title of this volume to describe the desire to bring this Bible topic to the table for new conversations, exploring how the holiness/sanctification message can be renewed for this day and the culture in which we live. The authors believe this exploration can be greatly aided by understanding the kind of Christian experiences that John Wesley's Methodists experienced, which were amazingly effective in transforming the culture of England in their day, as well as evangelizing the young nation called the United States of America. Those awakenings were quite impressive and effective in lifting the moral fiber of the entire culture. Today most Christians would agree that the United States and much of western culture need this once again.[7]

The thoughts in this volume are merely an attempt to start a conversation or to fan the flames of current conversations about the important role of sanctification in the life of believers. It aims to motivate Christians and aid them in advancing on their paths toward the image of Christ being formed in them and holy love filling them. This work hopes to offer seeds for potential solutions to the dilemma of the disappearance of sanctification from the minds of believers and from the pulpits of churches in America. The Bible affirms that the 'quest for holiness' offers untold benefits to individual lives, churches, the Christian Kingdom, even nations and cultures. Any call from God's eternal Word inherently holds blessings abundant when followed.

> Wherefore gird up the loins of your mind, be sober, and hope to the end for the grace that is to be brought unto you at the revelation of Jesus Christ; [14] As obedient children, not fashioning yourselves according to the former lusts in your ignorance: [15] But as he which hath called you is holy, so be ye holy in all manner of conversation; [16] Because it is written, Be ye holy; for I am holy (1 Pet. 1.13-16).

> For the grace of God that brings salvation has appeared to all men. [12] It teaches us to say 'No' to ungodliness and worldly passions, and to live self-controlled, upright and godly lives in this

---

[7] For this research data please see http://www.jesus-is-savior.com/Evils%20 in%20America/statistics.htm, also www.barna.org, and Jon Butler, Grant Wacker, and Randall Balmer, *Religion in American Life: A Short History* (Oxford/ New York: Oxford University Press, 2008).

present age, [13] while we wait for the blessed hope--the glorious appearing of our great God and Savior, Jesus Christ, [14] who gave himself for us to redeem us from all wickedness and to purify for himself a people that are his very own, eager to do what is good (Tit. 2.11-14 NIV).

I appeal to you therefore, brothers and sisters, by the mercies of God, to present your bodies as a living sacrifice, holy and acceptable to God, which is your spiritual worship. [2] Do not be conformed to this world, but be transformed by the renewing of your minds, so that you may discern what is the will of God – what is good and acceptable and perfect (Rom. 12.1-2 NRSV).

Voices with an Urgent Call

While doing research for this volume, voices were found sounding the alarm that the holiness of the Church is at a critical low and something must be done to awaken this essential nature of the Body of Christ. We must listen. Research and writing on holiness is short today and the words of J.I. Packer seem appropriate: 'Holiness is a neglected priority in the wider church and a faded glory among evangelicals'.[8]

David Peterson points out,

Very little attention is given to the subject [of holiness] in academic circles. Popular studies appear from time to time, lacking biblical insight and theological depth. Serious teaching about the theme is rarely heard in our churches. Meanwhile, much of contemporary church life seems superficial, self-indulgent and compromised.[9]

Scott Ellington says,

The company of biblical scholars engaging issues of holiness and sanctification is particularly select, and the conclave of Pentecostal biblical scholars who have taken up discussion of these crucial doctrines as we move into postmodern ethos is positively

---

[8] J.I. Packer, as quoted in David Peterson, *Possessed by God: A New Testament Theology of Sanctification and Holiness* (Grand Rapids, MI: Eerdmans, 1995), p. 18.

[9] David Peterson, *Possessed by God: A New Testament Theology of Sanctification and Holiness* (Grand Rapids, MI: Eerdmans, 1995), p. 18.

intimate … Silence on the topic of holiness and the Holy Spirit's role in bringing it to full harvest in the life of each believer, though, comes at a bad time. As the last vestiges of cultural Christianity begin to dissipate in the West and an individualistic syncretism of the heart becomes for many the greater moral good, we need with renewed energy and hunger to pursue Spirit-led holy lives.[10]

Daniel Castelo states, 'Holiness should be a part of Pentecostalism's future because it is so vital to Pentecostalism's past'. Yet when Castelo conversed with ministers asking, 'How does one come to be holy?', none gave an answer that was satisfactory. He found that a pattern emerged – they often shared that it was a very difficult matter, a complicated issue, and showed indecision or confusion, even disquietude related to the issue. Castelo was concerned that such a topic so basic to Pentecostal identity could be in such disarray. He thought, if Pentecostals are unable to articulate a theme so crucial to their past, then what hope exists for the tradition in terms of theological continuity.[11]

A.M. Hill observes,

Plainly there is no remedy but for the Church to come back to the very elements of piety. She must return to God and Holy Communion. The standard of piety must be raised. What can the Church do for the conversion of the world, for her own existence even, without personal holiness – much deep, pure, personal holiness? The standard of piety throughout the American Church is extremely and deplorably low. It is low compared with that of the primitive Church, compared with the provisions of the gospel, with the obligation of redeemed sinners, or with the requisite qualifications for the work to be done. The spirit of the

---

[10] Scott A. Ellington, 'Have We Been Sanctified?: Renewing the Role of Experience in Interpreting the Biblical Text', in Lee Roy Martin (ed.), *A Future for Holiness: Pentecostal Explorations* (Cleveland, TN: CPT Press, 2013), p. 109.

[11] Daniel Castelo, 'A Holy Reception Can Lead to a Holy Future', in Lee Roy Martin (ed.), *A Future for Holiness: Pentecostal Explorations* (Cleveland, TN: CPT Press, 2013), p. 227.

world has deeply pervaded and exceedingly engrossed the heart of the Church.[12]

A number of Pentecostal scholars (some of whom are ordained in classical Pentecostal churches) agree that holiness as it is lived by believers is facing challenges. David Daniels goes so far as to state that 'holiness has lost its currency among saints … It has been dismissed as suffocating. To be honest, there is no guarantee that holiness will even be of interest to the next generation; it might not even be a topic to discuss.'[13]

William Greathouse writes, 'How desperately we need such a vision of the Holy God in our day! In our culture a chatty familiarity with "the Man Upstairs" has displaced the speechless awe that dares not move in the presence of the Almighty'.[14]

Objectives

If these voices are on target, then the Church faces a huge challenge. As this book was under consideration, the question surfaced, 'What can help in this dilemma?' A strong sense of direction pointed back to the fountainhead of the modern-day holiness message, John Wesley. With that, these four objectives became clear. This volume aims to:

- Bring to pastors and leaders a taste of Wesley's vision and passion for holiness and sanctification, believing that it can still be contagious today;

- Speak a word into the advanced drift away from holiness and sanctification thought, teaching, preaching, and pursuit;

---

[12] A.M. Hill, *Holiness and Power for the Church and the Ministry* (New York: Garland Publishing, 1984), p. 19, as quoted in Antipas L. Harris, 'Holiness, the Church, and Party Politics: Toward A Contemporary Practical Theology of Holiness', in Lee Roy Martin (ed.), *A Future for Holiness: Pentecostal Explorations* (Cleveland, TN: CPT Press, 2013), pp. 265-66.

[13] David Daniels, as quoted by Marcia Clarke, 'A Future for Holiness in Pentecostal Practice', in Lee Roy Martin (ed.), *A Future for Holiness: Pentecostal Explorations* (Cleveland, TN: CPT Press, 2013), p. 350.

[14] William M. Greathouse, *Love Made Perfect: Foundations for the Holy Life* (Kansas City, MO: Beacon Hill, 1997), p. 28.

• Advance a conversation on how holiness and sanctification is a critical need of the Church and how it might be freshly packaged for a new day, new presentation, new culture, and new generation; and,

• Give practical applications/recommendations on how a pastor or leader could take steps to renew commitments to and pursuit of holiness and sanctification in the Church.

In Chapter 1, the word from Wesley is *motivation* as we consider Wesley's 'long view' for the salvation experience compared beside today's 'short view' and the general decrease of the life pursuit of holiness through sanctifying graces. In Chapter 2 the word from Wesley is *relation*, and we consider the foundation of holiness and all Christian life and growth is love, which continues today to be the greatest antidote for legalism, as well as license. In Chapter 3 the word from Wesley is *transformation*, and we look at Wesley's deep biblical conviction that the salvation journey was based on the presupposition that lives would be changed either in conversion, or in the sanctification process, or both, and rejecting that lives could remain as they were under the influence of grace. In Chapter 4 the word from Wesley is *formation*, and we investigate Wesley's commitment and genius to develop structure that facilitated the gracious sanctification/formation process. In Chapter 5 the word from Wesley is *mobilization*, and we discuss possibly the hidden gem of Methodism, the massive mobilization of believers to love God by loving others, especially in compassionate loving service to the needy. In Chapter 6 the word for today is *presentation* as we bring to the conversation ideas about new options for presenting the holiness/sanctification message in today's culture.

This volume is offered with this simple prayer: 'May the same grace that awakened the heart of John Wesley, awaken ministers, leaders, and believers once again to the high call of holiness'.

1

MOTIVATION

*In 1729, two young men, reading the Bible, saw that they could not be
saved without holiness, followed after it, and incited others to do so.*[1]
  — L.G. Cox (As they say, 'The rest is history!')

*Holiness can have a future in Pentecostalism only if the current-day
members of the tradition have the courage to recall and repair the way
holiness has been depicted in their past.*[2]   — Daniel Castelo

It has been well said that 'Holiness, to both John and Charles Wesley, was not a single narrow cultic idea. It was the whole point of the gospel'.[3] What has come to be known as the distinctive Wesleyan doctrine, entire sanctification, is really more of a recovery of an ancient patristic tradition. Yet it is properly perceived as a central feature of John Wesley's legacy.

Telos

It is possible that the best place to start an 'exploration for renewal in sanctification and holiness' would be with motivation. Wesley

---

[1] Leo George Cox, *John Wesley's Concept of Perfection* (Nicholasville, KY: Schmul Publishing, 1999), p. 7.
[2] Daniel Castelo, 'A Holy Reception Can Lead to a Holy Future', p. 234.
[3] Wilber T. Dayton, 'Entire Sanctification: The Divine Purification and Perfection of Man', in C.W. Carter, R.D. Thompson, and C.R. Wilson (eds.), *A Contemporary Wesleyan Theology: Biblical, Systematic, and Practical Volume One* (Grand Rapids: Zondervan, 1983), p. 522.

was motivated by the *'telos'* of salvation, the ultimate end goal.[4] He was passionate to help move believers ahead toward the purpose that God had in mind for those that would believe on him, follow him, and love him. For Wesley, that goal was the image of God, which was best described for him as holy love.[5]

Often translated 'perfection', the Greek *teleiotes* (τελειότης) is found in passages such as Col 3.14 and Heb. 6.1 and has been understood in terms of maturation and completeness. The Latin *perfectus*, from which many English speaking people draw their understanding of 'perfect', signifies a more static state without possibility of improvement (allowing no growth). However, *teleiotes* signifies a dynamic conception of that which is most excellent continuing in development (inviting growth). Here Wesley relied on the Greek text of the New Testament, not the Latin Vulgate or the English of the KJV. Thus, Wesley taught *perfecting* grace not *perfected* grace. This concept is frequently found in pre-Augustinian Eastern Church thinkers.

Wesley came to understand that justification was like the doorway into a house. Justification brought the believer through the door to enter the house, but it was sanctification that moved the believer through all of the rooms of the house so that the believer might inhabit all of them.[6] The house represented 'entire sanctification' for Wesley and a new convert should never be satisfied, or even left alone, to sit inside that doorway of mere conversion. The whole purpose of entering the house (salvation) was to discover and possess the rooms of purifying grace, holy love, and formation into the image of Christ. Wesley's house illustration paints the picture of his motivation concerning salvation. Simply entering the house through salvation by justification was far short of the goal of maturing to dwell in every room of the house in the fullness of salvation which God offers through sanctification to holiness.[7]

---

[4] Theodore Runyon, *The New Creation: John Wesley's Theology Today* (Nashville: Abingdon Press, 1998), p. 57.

[5] Dayton, 'Entire Sanctification: The Divine Purification and Perfection of Man', pp. 521-65. The overall chapter supports the teleological emphasis of John Wesley.

[6] Runyon, *The New Creation*, p. 27.

[7] John Wesley, 'The Principles of a Methodist Farther Explained', in John Wesley, *Works of the Rev. John Wesley* (London: Wesleyan Methodist Book Room,

Theodore Runyon observes, 'The anticipation of Christian perfection in this life was therefore a key element in Methodist piety and lent to it its distinctive character. The goal gave shape to the process. Remove this end and gradual transformation would be undercut as well.'[8] This is a profound quote as we look at the state of holiness and sanctification in our day, one hundred fifty years since the strength of the Holiness movement swept across the United States making its mark on nearly every kind of faith structure in existence then. Perhaps we can see in hindsight, the critical place 'the anticipation of Christian perfection' held.

Faith and Love

Wesley saw the 'focus' on the crisis faith experience of justification in his day as less helpful for continuing motivation than the more important goal of pursuing holy love, the image of Christ, and Christian perfection. Though history has made Wesley's Aldersgate experience a focal point with much attention given to that moment, it is interesting that Wesley did not. In his writing and speaking he points very little attention to what he experienced at Aldersgate. Some Wesleyan scholars believe it is not because the experience was diminished in Wesley's view, but they feel he did not want to give too much focus to the justifying experience of assurance he received there. He saw the justification experience receiving great attention in his day but he felt the people must be motivated onward to receive the call to a lifelong quest for holy love. In Wesley's view, justification was the entrance to the journey with much more to come. His passion was to bring people into the quest through justification, but to quickly show them their ultimate goal (Christian perfection) and encourage them immediately onward in their journey (Sanctification).

3rd edn, 1872), VIII, pp. 414-80. In this letter from 1746, Wesley stated, 'Our main doctrines, which include all the rest, are three, that of repentance, of faith, and of holiness. The first of these we account, as it were, the porch of religion; the next, the door; the third is religion itself' (p. 472). In addition, Robert Munger wrote an allegory, 'My Heart Christ's Home', which captures this Wesleyan concept effectively. Written in 1951 it can now be found in many locations online. http://www.usna.edu/Navigators/_files/documents/ MHCH. pdf The US Naval Academy, The Navigators ministry page, accessed March 2016.

[8] Runyon, *The New Creation*, p. 97.

The focus was on faith in the justifying experience, but Wesley felt the greater motivation for pursuing the image of God was love. With faith as the motivation, the focus lay on believing all that Christ had done for fallen humanity. Once that faith was embraced, the pardon was received and all was well. This left believers with only the motivation to maintain their faith and wait for the Kingdom to come. Writers from Luther's day until Wesley expressed this mundane view as the normal expectation for believers. Naturally, Wesley was not satisfied with that perspective and felt there was much more that God intended for believers.

We can see the same tendencies among believers today. Salvation is presented as a onetime act of faith that secures pardon for our sins and assurance of heaven beyond this life. Once those two graces have been received by faith there is little to motivate believers onward to pursue more in Christ. Now they can wait in peace knowing that they are a child of God and have the hope of heaven. Today churches are filled with passive believers who have never been challenged to more or who have heard challenges to higher life but feel little motivation to leave their comfort zone of faith to reach up for greater grace and life.

For reasons such as these, Wesley believed that love was the better center for the Christian life. Crisis moment faith provided salvation blessings but with no continuing motivation for Christian growth. Love for God, on the other hand, was born in the heart of believers at justification and the new birth, but it had all the potential to grow in limitless measure as the believer experienced more and more of God through the diverse means of grace. Faith also was easily confined in Wesley's day (as well as our own) to the realm of the mind – intellectual assent. This disturbed Wesley because he saw churches filled with nominal Christians who gave intellectual assent to the tenants of the faith, yet their lives were never impacted or changed by the gospel knowledge they seemingly held. Wesley felt that the shift from crisis faith to love, or from the mind to the heart, would help lead believers away from nominal Christian practice and into heartfelt 'orthopathy' – right passions.

Wesley was living in the threshold of change philosophically on how experience was viewed. He personally saw scriptural evidence that believers could and should have emotive and sensory experience that accompanied their faith. The fruit of the Spirit would certainly qualify as a primary example: love, joy, and peace are each a feeling that the Bible ascribes to the work of the Spirit. So Wesley took his cue from John Locke who was leading an element of this philosophical shift. Locke believed that experience was a reliable source of knowledge and gave it a place of authority alongside scripture, tradition, and reason.[9]

With the help of Locke's writing, Wesley now had a foundation to thrust into new frontiers for the Kingdom of God. Dogmatic orthodoxy had ruled the day for centuries, the idea that right belief (mental assent) described correct faith. Wesley, however, felt that right belief should be expressed in right practice (orthopraxy), and he pressed for Christian experience that transformed the life of the believer. But Wesley also knew that right practice (orthopraxy) nor right belief (orthodoxy) alone could guarantee true transforming faith. For Wesley, the heart was the critical element, and he saw in the Bible the reality that the Spirit of God could transform the heart bringing right passions, orthopathy. Wesley is credited as the first to weave the experiential nature of faith into his theology and Christian practice, building on orthodoxy, to orthopraxy, and to orthopathy. In effect Wesley shifted the center for his Methodist movement from faith to the heart, from mental assent to holy love.[10]

Legalism and Little Interest

We think most would agree with The Barna Group above, that far too many believers today simply do not care about pursuing holiness. We would like to consider briefly a few reasons why people may feel this way. For earlier generations of holiness people, there could be the baggage of legalism that they witnessed or heard about in their own churches through the years gone by. It is regrettable

---

[9] Runyon, *The New Creation*, p. 73. Wesley used these four categories in the well-known 'Wesleyan Quadrilateral': Scripture, Tradition, Reason, and Experience.

[10] Steven J. Land, *Pentecostal Spirituality: A Passion for the Kingdom* (JPTSup 1; Sheffield, UK: Sheffield Academic Press, 1993), pp. 41-46. Land speaks of the interaction between beliefs, actions, and affections and provides a broad discussion for this synthesis.

that anyone would abandon the 'quest for holiness', which is so clearly depicted in Scripture, because they have seen others twist the motivation into perverted forms. That is indeed sad, and it is a real challenge we face today. Theologian Steve Land has stated, when asked about this baggage of legalism, 'What legalism? All I see today is license!'[11] Land affirms that the legalism excuse is in reality a critique of past decades, while having lesser relevance to the present conversation of renewal of the holiness/sanctification message.

Yes, it is an obvious fact that, in most Holiness movements of the mid 1900's, they gave so much attention to external measurements for holiness that the entire movement was greatly drawn away from the most significant core values. Those core values would have included emulating the image of Christ, being filled with the holy love of God, participating in the many means of grace to mature in holiness, and walking in the Spirit toward the goal of entire sanctification. With the rise of the focus on externals, the holiness movement generally was drawn away from its Wesleyan roots. Holiness became more about how a believer looked and acted in observable criteria than it was about true life transformation and the entrance into an intimate life and walk with Christ by the Spirit in love. Legalism must be a caution to avoid in any current renewal of the holiness message, but today most must agree with Steve Land that it is far overshadowed by license.

Mental Assent

It can safely be said that many believers do not care to pursue holiness because they are saved and on their way to heaven, which is really all that matters to them anyway. This 'saved to wait' or 'saved to sit' mentality has been greatly encouraged by the way salvation has been presented to masses in our time and earlier. Numerous illustrations can be drawn from the last fifty years demonstrating how salvation has been presented and accepted by the lost as a decision of the moment where they accepted or declared their agreement that Jesus died for their sins. Mass crusades, revival meetings,

---

[11] Steve Land, 'Renewal in Holiness'. This presentation was made to the International Assembly of the Church of God of Prophecy in 2012 in Nashville, TN.

personal evangelism encounters, to name only a few, would all ascribe to this presentation of salvation.

For many, salvation over these years could easily be received by simply giving mental assent to the fact that Jesus was the Christ and that he offers salvation to all that believe. Since saving faith was presented as a step of simple mental assent, nothing else was expected, and these believers were then ready for heaven when their time came.[12] All that seemed to be expected was to wait. In this approach, there is little if any motivation for a life-consuming quest for something beyond initial salvation, a journey that would demand every ounce of their will and effort. That would seem superfluous.

More recently there have been attempts to make churches more open and receptive to the lost of their communities. In this very worthy effort, there has possibly been an unintentional adaptation to this presentation of salvation that seems to attempt to make the threshold for salvation as low or as easy as possible. If before, the salvation presentation was saying, 'Come to Jesus, it is simple', now the message would seem to come across as, 'Come to Jesus as you are, and remain as you are' (the implicit message).

Once again the spirit of Wesley has not only been shifted, it has literally been reversed. As we have stated, Wesley's attitude was to call people from the very beginning to the life-long journey of holiness/sanctification. The findings of a study done of hundreds of new believers' testimonies found in Wesley's regular publication, *The Arminian Magazine* is enlightening here. Of over 400 testimonies studied, it was only after over two years of participation in Wesley's network of small group growth and Christian development that the average participant was converted to Christ. Surely that is clear evidence that Wesley built his movement based on the long-range motivation of growing in the holiness/sanctification process more than on the immediate crisis moment of belief in Jesus Christ. We can add to this the report that Wesley often gave his call to the people after preaching in the open fields to hundreds and thousands, not as an invitation to come and receive Christ, but as an invitation

---

[12] Runyon, *The New Creation*, p. 58. See also pp 85, 142.

to go, attend, and join one of the local small groups, societies, classes, or bands, in the community.[13] Clearly, Wesley demonstrates a radically different motivation than we have seen develop in the last one hundred years in Protestant Christianity. Given the dilemma we face in the western world today, perhaps it is time to give serious consideration to Wesley's view of initial motivation as we attempt to make new converts.

Finished Work

The 'finished work' doctrine with its family of modifications helps believers settle into all that God has done for them, without worrying too much about what God may want to do in them and through them by his Spirit. When Wesley visited Hernhut, Zinzendorf of the Moravians said, 'Our whole justification and sanctification are in the same instant and the believer receives neither more nor less'.[14] This concept is called 'finished work' theology today. If one can receive no more through arduous seeking than one already has, then why bother? In contrast, Wesley wanted to challenge his followers to not only answer the question, 'Am I saved?' but to also seek to answer the question, 'For what purpose am I saved?'[15]

Wesley and George Whitfield had intense debates and conflict over their differing views of the finished work doctrine and Wesleyan Arminianism. Ultimately they 'agreed to disagree'. The anecdotal quote from George Whitfield helps us see his grace to appreciate Wesley's ministry and movement despite their deep differences. Someone asked Whitfield if John Wesley would be in heaven. Whitfield paused and answered, 'I doubt that we will be able to see Mr. Wesley in heaven; he will be so far in the distance up near to the throne of God and Jesus Christ'. The followers of these two leaders also struggled intensely between one another all through Wesley's days and beyond. Wesley's most well known follower, who was actually intended to succeed Wesley as the leader of the movement, John Fletcher, said that his main work had been the defense

---

[13] Runyon, *The New Creation*, p. 115.
[14] Kenneth J. Collins, *John Wesley: A Theological Journey* (Nashville: Abingdon Press, 2003), p. 113.
[15] Chilcote, *Recapturing the Wesleys' Vision*.

of Arminianism under the attack of the finished work proponents.[16] This describes the tensions that these two views generated as far back as the 1700's.

Today we see an unintended result of finished work teaching at the grass roots. There are new converts and other believers that approach deception when they find it easy to believe that once they are saved, justified, and decreed holy before God, they are free to sin with no ramifications, or even at times with no remorse. They have been taught that the work of justification is so sure and unchangeable that it does not matter what they may do, including sin. There can be no doubt that it is certainly not the aim of any finished work theologian, but the finished work teaching opens up the possibility for thinking such as this. Wesley called this line of thought 'antinomianism', (the state of being without law) and rejected it vigorously throughout his ministry.[17] Obviously one can easily see that this line of thinking would have a negative impact on the motivation to grow in holiness through sanctification by the Spirit toward the image of Christ. Again, they might say logically, 'Why bother?'

Nobody's Perfect

We suggest that the question of motivation is critical to the popular phrase used by believers today, 'Nobody's perfect!' We hear this so often it causes us to ask, 'Is anyone pursuing Christian perfection or is everyone satisfied with, "Nobody's perfect?"' Some may not realize there is a big difference. We have always heard that if you aim for the moon you might at least escape the atmosphere. For us, that seems to be the difference between aiming for Wesley's Christian perfection (the image of Christ) and settling for 'Nobody's per-

---

[16] Matthew K. Thompson, 'John Fletcher's Trinitarian Theology of Grace', in Henry H. Knight III (ed.), *From Aldersgate to Azusa Street: Wesleyan, Holiness, and Pentecostal Visions of the New Creation* (Eugene, OR: Pickwick Publications, 2010), pp. 33-35.

[17] I. Howard Marshall, *1 Peter* (IVPNTC; Downers Grove: Intervarsity Press, 1991), p. 54. Marshall supports Wesley as he comments on 1 Pet. 1.17 saying, 'Christians are not in a position where it doesn't matter how they live because they believe in Christ and all will be forgiven at the last judgment. On the contrary they should live in this world, filled with its temptations, with reverence for God in the face of his judgment.'

fect' (sin a little now and then). When we settle for 'Nobody's perfect', it seems that all motivation for reaching the heights is lost. It leaves so much room for low expectations or no expectations and certainly gives no motivation for striving for and attaining something glorious.

William Greathouse has a contribution to make on this idea, 'Nobody's Perfect!':

> All their lives people have been dismissing their moral failures with this worldly dictum. But that notion does not come from the Bible. The Holy Scriptures are not bashful in calling God's people to perfection ... How desperately we need such a vision of the Holy God in our day! In our culture a chatty familiarity with 'the Man Upstairs' has displaced the speechless awe that dares not move in the presence of the Almighty.[18]

We are afraid that Christianity today has bought into the bumper sticker doctrine of 'Nobody's perfect' and have missed the thrill and life-consuming challenge of giving our all to aim for Christian perfection. It is an exciting adventure to awake each day with the aim of 'being with God' through his Word, through his Spirit, through his people, and through joining him in acts of mercy or piety that day. The conviction here is like that of Isaiah, Job, and John the Revelator; we believe that getting in God's presence brings transformation. Isn't that one of the lessons to be learned from Moses' experience with God on Mount Sinai? Moses had spent time in God's presence; and, when he came down, he was aglow from associating with God in his glory. The holiness/sanctification journey intends a life that aims to be in God's presence as often as possible so that this kind of transformation can take place often. 'From glory to glory' is the biblical phrase that hints at the promise that repeated moments in his presence will move us from glory to glory, toward the image of Christ (2 Cor. 3.18). That is a fundamental motivation of holiness/sanctification.

Yes, this conversation quickly gets pulled down into the questions, 'What is perfect?', or 'Who is perfect?', or "Is perfection possible?' But that was the genius of John Wesley. He continued to draw attention back to the 'pursuit' of holy love, the journey, and

---

[18] Greathouse, *Love Made Perfect: Foundations for the Holy Life*, pp. 34, 28.

the passion for going on toward attaining such a prize. Wesley would not be distracted by the question of defining perfection and nailing it down to how many angels can dance on the head of a pin.[19] The calls from God's Word were sufficient and strong enough to convince Wesley that this was not only a goal worthy of Christian focus, but it was 'the great goal' of Christian calling. Yes, to Wesley the great cause was not to be saved, but to accept the noble and high call to become like Christ and to be filled with his Holy love.

Motivation was the key for Wesley and must be for us today. Again, let us ask, rephrased: 'Which of you is pouring all of your energy into being like Jesus every day and believes it is a goal worthy of your life, blood, sweat, and tears? Or who is satisfied to live making the excuse, "Nobody's perfect?"' Some are going to aim for soaring with the eagles (Isa. 40.28), while many are going to settle for hanging around with the turkeys. The choice is ours.[20] Of course there are many resting points between those two poles where believers have taken up refuge believing they have gone far enough; they become fatigued or feel they do not know how to go any further. Once more this was the genius of Wesley; he offered biblical paths for believers to use to help them continue on the journey of holiness with far less premature derailments. This volume will discuss these paths in Chapter 4, but it is safe to say right now as we speak of motivations and the demise of the holiness/sanctification message, one can find today only a rare few motivational paths offering guidance and help to facilitate one's journey toward this great goal. Search as you may, a dismal few efforts can be found that invest great energy to provide such guidance, beyond the common norm of attend church, give, study with us in Sunday school, or in

---

[19] Even in his famous treatise on Christian Perfection, Wesley *described* perfection rather than *defined* it. In other words, rather than offer a technical or speculative definition – some kind of theological formula – Wesley described perfection in biblical and historical language with demonstrable ethical and moral applications. In a sense, Wesley offered a portrait of Christian perfection more than anything else. See John Wesley, 'A Plain Account of Christian Perfection, as Believed and Taught by the Reverend Mr. John Wesley, from the Year 1725, to the Year 1777', in *Works of the Rev. John Wesley*, XI, pp. 366-445.

[20] Jim Wallis, 'Can You Really Tell a Difference?', online citation May 15, 2015, http://sojo.net/blogs/2013/09/26/can-you-really-tell-difference-between-christians-and-non-christians. If anyone has doubts about the 'nobody's perfect' motivational drain going on today, just read this online blog and see how boldly the challenge goes out to NOT promote Christian perfection.

less cases meet with a small group that is not designed for this journey either. For anyone that is interested, Wesley offers words of tried and practiced success to help. It is the intent of this volume to lead others into these words and the conversation of application for renewal of the holiness/sanctification message so greatly needed today.

The Long View of Salvation

When one realizes Wesley's view of salvation was from the 'Big Picture' perspective it is easy to see why he was not satisfied with preaching and leading people to small 's' salvation, the decision of the moment to believe on Christ and receive forgiveness. For Wesley, salvation was the long journey of life, being formed in the image of God (Gal. 4.19) through his grace and the person of the Holy Spirit, perfecting holiness in the fear of God (2 Cor. 7.1). With this view, Wesley was eager to call his followers onward beyond the moment of small 'j' justification (which was the 'big deal' in his day) and thrust ahead toward holy love, the image of God, entire sanctification, and yes, Christian perfection.[21]

Some reflect that Wesley never made much of his Aldersgate conversion in his writings or preaching because he did not want to over emphasize his experience of assurance in justification and diminish the call and motivation to keep walking on toward the ultimate goal of the image of Christ.[22] It is interesting that today Christianity seems to be doing the opposite, we make conversion everything and find that no one wants to pursue discipleship or sanctification or holiness further.

Wesley was drawn and motivated by scriptural calls to this 'long view' of salvation, such as:

[11] The gifts he gave were that some would be apostles, some prophets, some evangelists, some pastors and teachers, [12] to equip the saints for the work of ministry, for building up the body of Christ, [13] until all of us come to the unity of the faith and of the knowledge of the Son of God, to maturity, to the

---

[21] Cox, *John Wesley's Concept of Perfection*, p. 7.
[22] Runyon, *The New Creation*, p. 49.

measure of the full stature of Christ. [14] We must no longer be children, tossed to and fro and blown about by every wind of doctrine, by people's trickery, by their craftiness in deceitful scheming. [15] But speaking the truth in love, we must grow up in every way into him who is the head, into Christ, [16] from whom the whole body, joined and knit together by every ligament with which it is equipped, as each part is working properly, promotes the body's growth in building itself up in love (Eph. 4.11-16 (NRSV).

Wesley adopted the ministry philosophy that as he aimed to guide everyone toward this high goal, the people would receive Christ and Christ's justifying work in good time and on the way. The comparison of the two philosophies might be similar to calling a group of people together and telling them that in time everyone was going to run a marathon. The group then goes about to accomplish that very difficult task. In comparison, a group is called together and told that today they are going to run a mile. But at the end of the mile the leader tries to encourage them that they can run another mile, and then another, and another with those few that are willing to go on with him. No doubt by the end of the third or fourth mile everyone would drop out because that is not, at all, what they signed on for. They had no idea the leader intended, in his own mind, to motivate them on to run a marathon that day.

When the difference in the current day 'short view' of salvation and Wesley's 'long view' of salvation are compared in a simple illustration like this, it becomes obvious that logic is missing in the 'short view' approach. Yet we must confess that this is the general way the protestant faith has been operating now for many years. One can easily ask, 'Is it any wonder that believers do not rate any different than non-believers in polls that evaluate actual behaviors today?' Like the bumper sticker says proudly, 'I am not perfect, just forgiven'.

We know that Evangelical Christianity in the last one hundred years has felt that bringing salvation to lost people and lifting them from sin's condemnation was judged more important than the 'long view' approach. On the other hand, by aiming for the high goal, Wesley did a great work bringing lost people to Christ AND form-

ing them into a nation shaking movement with this philosophy. Today may be the time for a reevaluation since after decades on this
road in the west, we neither have a nation shaking movement nor
growing masses of lost people coming to Christ.[23]

Dumbed Down Salvation

As this holiness/sanctification conversation progresses it would
seem that there has been an attempt to lower the threshold of salvation as well as to lower the life-walking expectations as a believer
in general.[24] Could it be we have 'dumbed down' Christianity and
now we are getting the fruit of such a faith? Anything that seems
to be hard, or that might smack against cultural sensitivities, or that
might be politically incorrect, or religiously incorrect, many today
want to leave that out of the faith. In a conversation between co-
author Tony Richie and David Roebuck, Director of the Dixon
Pentecostal Research Center, Dr. Roebuck mentioned the hypothesis that taking holiness and sanctification out of the Pentecostal
journey may have contributed to the attrition of those seeking and
experiencing Spirit Baptism.[25] After all, the Pentecostal Movement
sprang out of the Holiness Movement where believers were pas-
sionately seeking a deeper experience and genuine purity of life.
This may or may not be validated through research, but it seems far
more certain that deleting preaching and teaching about holiness
and sanctification will indeed lead to believers that lack any motivation to pursue, diligently and with vigor, a life filled with love, or a
life walking in victory over obvious sin, or a life clearly growing to
look more and more like Christ. It seems improbable, but the reality
appears to be that many believe holiness will remain intact without

---

[23] See http://evangelicalarminians.org/john-wesley/and https://www.nph.
com/vcmedia/2419/2419619.pdf for further discussion on this 'long view' of
salvation that Wesley embraced with deep conviction (accessed Dec. 31, 2015).

[24] J. Ayodeji Adewuya, *Holiness in the Letters of Paul: The Necessary Response to the
Gospel* (Eugene, OR: Cascade, 2016), p. 163, writes: 'Until we reach heaven, there
is always a higher level of the Christian life to be experienced. Because of this
reality, each believer should strive daily to grow further in holiness.'

[25] David Roebuck, personal conversation with Tony Richie and Randy Howard after a lecture by Dr. Richie on Wesleyan Theology at the Pentecostal Theological Seminary, May 2015, Cleveland, TN. Dr. Roebuck is an academic historian
focusing his study on the Pentecostal Movement.

preaching and teaching about it, or calling people to moments of sanctification and consecration. 'Go Figure!'

Righteous Indignation

Another motivation for Wesley was his keen dissatisfaction with religion as he saw it during his lifetime. Nominalism was the order of the day. Assent to the tenants of the faith as held in the Church of England was all that was necessary. This can be seen in the tongue-in-cheek line that Wesley gave to a distracter when challenged with sacrilege for using lay preachers to spread the gospel and call people to faith outside the hallowed walls of the Church. Wesley said, 'Is not a lay preacher preferable to a drunken preacher, to a cursing, swearing preacher?'[26] If this was the view from the pulpit in the Church of England, then we can assume more of the same from the pew in Wesley's day.

Now considering our own day and culture, we sense a similar rising tide of dissatisfaction from Christian leaders and believers generally.[27] Perhaps a swelling motivation is on the rise for a renewal of holiness and the call to sanctified experience. In the current day, righteous indignation may not be the correct response, though it seems clear some response is needed. As so many statistical reports mark the lack of progress for Christianity in America it could be that the first response would be to set aside the 'poker face' or façade designed to make everything appear to be in order and flowing smoothly. Is that a biblical response? The more common biblical response would be to cry out to God, call for a 'solemn assembly', and seek his intervention for an Awakening. A second response can be seen clearly in Wesley's life and ministry. He methodically (Methodists) went about the business of designing a new approach to ministry that carried the gospel effectively in a new environment, that targeted the most needy and massive segments of society, that

---

[26] Collins, *John Wesley*, p. 109. See also Steve Harper, *The Way to Heaven* (Grand Rapids, MI: Zondervan, 2003), p. 106.

[27] Runyon, *The New Creation*, p. 168. Runyon says, 'When Christian perfection becomes the goal, a fundamental hope is aroused that the future can surpass the present. And a corresponding holy 'dissatisfaction' is aroused with regard to any present state of affairs, a dissatisfaction that supplies the critical edge necessary to keep the process of individual transformation moving.'

introduced a structure to maintain those that were drawn into this ministry, and that mobilized the majority of those attracted right back into service of some kind.

The Quest for Holiness

Perhaps the time is near, when the Holy Spirit will empower many to 'blow the trumpet in Zion'. He is the sanctifying Spirit, and he can call the Church back to her pursuit of the holiness of God! Yes, we see such clearly in scripture:

> [9] ... and be found in him, not having a righteousness of my own that comes from the law, but one that comes through faith in Christ, the righteousness from God based on faith. [10] I want to know Christ and the power of his resurrection and the sharing of his sufferings by becoming like him in his death, [11] if somehow I may attain the resurrection from the dead. [12] Not that I have already obtained this or have already reached the goal; but I press on to make it my own, because Christ Jesus has made me his own. [13] Beloved, I do not consider that I have made it my own; but this one thing I do: forgetting what lies behind and straining forward to what lies ahead, [14] I press on toward the goal for the prize of the heavenly call of God in Christ Jesus (Phil. 3.9-14 NRSV).

> [20] Now the God of peace, that brought again from the dead our Lord Jesus, that great shepherd of the sheep, through the blood of the everlasting covenant, [21] Make you perfect in every good work to do his will, working in you that which is well pleasing in his sight, through Jesus Christ; to whom *be* glory for ever and ever. Amen (Heb. 13.20-21).

In summary for this segment on Motivation and with application in view, what is the goal of salvation? If the goal of salvation is something far greater than merely being forgiven and heaven-ready, then what must be done? What does the Bible say here? If our goal as a believer is to love God and others with all that is within us, how should our religious practices change to reflect that purpose? If our goal is to become like Christ, in his image, then what can we do today and this week to draw closer to such an amazing goal?

Is it good enough for believers to be satisfied with the excuse, 'Nobody's Perfect?', or is being filled with God's love to such an extent that our lives are transformed and Christ is seen more clearly just a Don Quixote dream from La Mancha? Are we dreaming the impossible dream, or is God calling us to something glorious and far beyond our capabilities through our own strength?

Are we as believers on a long march to the 'promised land', or are we stuck in 'Haran', where we left our home in the world and now seems to be marooned, or worse, wandering about aimlessly in the wilderness. Has God's intention in this 'great salvation' been 'dumbed down' for easier access, and now we see there are consequences for that approach? Does anyone feel something like Jesus felt, 'righteous indignation', when we see the gospel in decline in our culture, evil abounding, and believers impotent to respond? Dr. Chris Green said,

> Pentecostals have a long history of talking about holiness. But it is at too many places a tragic history, a history of contradiction and failed promises. For sure, as heirs of the Wesleyan legacy, we should be thankful for the insistence that 'holiness is integral to the Christian life'. But we also should realize the time has come for an across-the-board, to-the-root revisioning. Daniel Castelo, I think, has it right: 'holiness can have a future in Pentecostalism only if the current-day members of the tradition have the courage to recall and repair the way holiness has been depicted in their past.'[28]

Applications

Our efforts when converting the lost must call for more than mental assent. With the model of Wesley, we have the privilege to call people to join the grand march toward the image of Christ formed in their lives. There will be more discussion on how to do this during the course of this book. This recommendation calls for a commitment, a complete buy-in, to the philosophy of the 'long view' of salvation. This commitment also includes the commitment that

---

[28] Chris Green, *Sanctifying Interpretation: Vocation, Holiness and Scripture* (Cleveland, TN: CPT Press, 2015), p. 64.

more ministry must be added to the experience of mental assent in order to assure new converts are engaged in processes for Christian development (See Chapter 4).

Making the further 'order of salvation' clear to new converts as early as possible would help in avoiding a 'one and done' mentality, as well as encouraging them toward greater things ahead. This means a more intentional effort must be made to relate with new converts and to mentor, coach, and motivate them (See Chapter 4).

If the assumption is true that the holiness/sanctification thrust has fallen through the cracks even among Holiness movements, then one recommendation would be that those who feel this passion ought to begin to preach, teach, and speak about it much more often to help raise the message back up to the table. Perhaps Wesley's attitude could encourage us as he said, 'all our Preachers should make a point of preaching perfection to believers constantly, strongly, and explicitly; and all believers should mind this one thing, and continually agonize for it'.[29] Though we may repackage it from Wesley's 'perfection' label, his advice is sound for ministers with a God given inspiration to lift the holiness message once again. Consider an intentional cyclical approach to help to keep these truths in view for all.

We must make it clear that the holiness we seek is first and foremost a matter of the heart, continuing to denounce all types of legalism derived from works righteousness, as well as denouncing the antinomianism in license. As we confront both fallacies, we understand that we do not want to fall back into the legalism of the past, and neither do we want to encourage antinomian trends of the present. We believe the foundation of love forms the best and most biblical context for pursuing the holiness/sanctification message once again (See Chapter 2).

Antinomianism, that is, lawlessness, was a lifelong concern for John Wesley. While many are concerned (rightly enough) with legalism, or attempts at salvation by keeping the law, Wesley greatly

---

[29] John Wesley, *A Plain Account of Christian Perfection* (Peabody, MA: Hendrikson, 2007), p. 119, as quoted by Brandon B. Smith in 'John Wesley's Christian Perfection: Myths, Realities, and Critique', accessed online May 15, 2015 in Patheos Conversations on Faith, http://www.patheos.com/blogs/brandondsmith/2015/03/john-wesleys-christian-perfection-myths-realities-and-critique/#ixzz 3XrXKaxdK.

feared the equal and opposite danger of flaunting disregard for God's enduring moral law. His doctrine of sanctification meant to counter that problem. Of course, there have been godly Christians across the spectrum of particular beliefs and traditions. There is no suggestion that only those who formally adhere to entire sanctification will live holy lives. However, the idea that 'nobody's perfect' or that 'everyone sins more or less every day' can certainly undermine the intensity and urgency of one's pursuit of holiness, even among the best of believers. Among some it might conceivably contribute to tragic complacency regarding personal godliness and righteousness, for others it may even foster antinomianism. This must be challenged by Christian leaders everywhere.

It will be a benefit to keep the goal in mind for believers by speaking often, if not weekly, about our journey to 'put on Christ', his love, his image, his purity, and his compassion. Paint the picture often for believers as to what a believer looks like that is walking in holy love, expressing the image of Christ. It is believed that Wesley grew so weary of questions about the definition of 'perfection', that he chose instead to paint the verbal picture of purity, giving biblical descriptions of the life of purity.[30]

To break through the disinterest in pursuing a holy life and the stages of sanctification involved, it would be helpful to hold consecration services or weave the call to consecration, surrender, and self evaluation frequently into the annual church service calendar as well as the regular prayer calls.

Intentionally break the 'nobody's perfect' hold on believers today by continuously promoting and calling people to the 'higher calling' of the pursuit for holiness, the quest for the image of Christ and holy love. Help believers join the march toward the glory of God rather than being content to sit on their salvation or imperfections. Imperfection is not the problem. Living contentedly in imperfection, satisfied that nothing better is expected, is a great problem.

Rather than 'dumbing down' salvation and the Christian life, strategically raise the threshold so that believers know their church strives to develop believers that are passionate for Christ and his

---

[30]This is clearly seen in Wesley's 'Plain Account of Christian Perfection'. A segment of this sermon is quoted in Chapter 3.

cause, pursuing holiness through the Spirit as their primary aim in life.

New convert counseling (one on one) and/or new believer groups would be a good way to present the larger vision of salvation and encourage these believers to join others in a pursuit for God. Later we will see that having a concrete structure or track to invite them to participate in will be of great value (See Chapter 4).

The target here is not only the new believer. This message should be used to awaken the nominal and satisfied believers in every church and mobilize them as well. Paul's call to apprehend this treasure is for everyone (Phil. 3.10-14).

One recommendation could be taken directly from the words of Robert C. Crosby's article on 'Joshua's Holy Ground Experience'. The main idea seems to be that God wanted to deal with the leader's sanctity 'before' he was interested in giving him the strategy for battle and victory. Our application for today could be that we have been more interested in seeking the newest fad strategies for ministry and may have overlooked and left undone the primary quest for holiness. The recommendation would then be to make the pursuit of personal holiness the highest priority, even 'before' ministry strategies and promotions.[31]

If the call is as urgent as the sources indicate, then it seems in order for Christian leaders to follow Daniel's and Jeremiah's examples to cry out and weep over the apathy toward and even the loss of this central Bible message. Moving one step further, if Dr. David Roebuck is correct and the loss of the holiness/sanctification message has subtly dulled our hunger for the fullness of the Holy Spirit, as well as opened the door for complacency in pursuing the 'higher life', then who will kneel under the call of the Spirit to repent for the holiness church, asking for God to 'hear from heaven' in mercy? A.M. Hill observes:

> Plainly there is no remedy but for the Church to come back to the very elements of piety. She must return to God and to Holy Communion. The standard of piety must be raised. What can

---

[31] Robert C. Crosby, 'Joshua's Holy Ground Experience', in Lee Roy Martin (ed.), *A Future for Holiness: Pentecostal Explorations* (Cleveland, TN: CPT Press, 2013), p. 24.

the Church do for the conversion of the world, for her own existence even, without personal holiness – much deep, pure, personal holiness. The standard of piety throughout the American Church is extremely and deplorably low. It is low compared with that of the primitive church, compared with the provisions of the gospel, with the obligation of redeemed sinners, or with the requisite qualifications for the work to be done. The spirit of the world has deeply pervaded and exceedingly engrossed the heart of the Church.[32]

John Wesley's Prayer

Pardon, good Lord, all my former sins, and make me every day more zealous and diligent

to improve every opportunity of building up my soul in Your faith, love, and obedience.

Make Yourself present always to my mind, and let Your love fill and rule in all places, company, and work to which You call me this day. Amen.[33]

I rejoice in the beginnings of that heavenly life which I feel in my heart. I myself have tasted the consolation and comfort in the fellowship of the Spirit; this makes me sensitive to the needs of others.

I earnestly desire that Your love come to perfection in me so that more and more the narrowness of my spirit may change to a larger and larger outlook on all human beings. Amen.[34]

---

[32] Hill, *Holiness and Power for the Church and the Ministry*, p. 19.

[33] Prayers excerpted from John Wesley, *Wesley's Daily Prayers: Prayers for Every Day in the Year* (ed. Donald E. Demaray; Anderson, IN: Bristol House, 1998), p. 35.

[34] Wesley, *Wesley's Daily Prayers*, p. 74.

2

RELATION

The best of all, God is with us.[1] – John Wesley's last words.

Thou madest us for thyself, and our heart is restless, until it repose in thee.[2] – Augustine

The summarizing word – Wesley's ultimate hermeneutic – is love. Every strand of his thought, the warm heart of every doctrine, the passion of every sermon, the test of every claim to Christian grace, was love. So central is love that to be 'Wesleyan' is to be committed to a theology of love.[3] – Mildred Bangs Wynkoop

The Relational Key

After the Church considers how she can best motivate believers and new converts up and onward with a hunger for the holy love of God, the second step the Church must make, if not a concomitant step, is to recast the doctrine of holiness as relational. Wesley reconceived the process of salvation as a relationship with God![4] His life had tested this hypothesis right in the middle of an age where

---

[1] Runyon, *The New Creation: John Wesley's Theology Today*, p. 101.
[2] Greathouse, *Love Made Perfect: Foundations for the Holy Life*, p. 103.
[3] Mildred Bangs Wynkoop, *A Theology of Love: The Dynamic of Wesleyanism* (Kansas City, MO: Beacon Hill, 1972), p. 76.
[4] Chilcote, *Recapturing the Wesleys' Vision*, p. 29.

the Church was embarrassingly nominal, with interest in the sacraments low,[5] and drunken, swearing preachers[6] known publicly.

Here is one description of Wesley's day which demonstrates that
it was not dissimilar to our own:

> Eighteenth-century England was a vest-pocket edition of today's
> cynical world. It helped to imprison love in 'low' forms unre-
> deemed by love's 'higher' relationships. It glorified a cruel, vul-
> gar, sodden life-style reaching from the palace down to the low-
> est level of society. In it, human life had little value and no mean-
> ing. It is significant that in that age of unrestrained permissive-
> ness – called love – John Wesley, the modern 'Apostle of Love',
> should have appeared. He proclaimed holiness, the highest pos-
> sible spiritual value, in terms of love, in the face of love's lowest
> possible connotation.[7]

In such a low tide of faith Wesley found models of relational
spirituality in the Bible and the early church Fathers that challenged
him. At Oxford as a young man with his 'holy club', Wesley devoted
himself to a new consecration of faith and seeking.

> I resolve to dedicate all my life to God, all my thoughts and
> words and actions, being thoroughly convinced there was no
> medium, but that every part of my life (not only some) must
> either be a sacrifice to God, or to myself; that is, in effect, to the
> devil ... I determined, through his grace (the absolute necessity
> of which I was deeply sensible of) to be all devoted to God.[8]

Wesley realized the Christian life is essentially a way of devotion.

Mildred Bangs Wynkoop is a Wesleyan Holiness Theologian. In
her work, *A Theology of Love*, she speaks of the love center of the
holiness/sanctification message which Wesley espoused:

> Love is so central to Christian faith that to touch it is to find
> oneself entangled with every element of Christian doctrine and
> life ... Wesley's discussions of any segment of Christian truth

---

[5] Chilcote, *Recapturing the Wesleys' Vision*, p. 84.

[6] Collins, *John Wesley: A Theological Journey*, p. 109.

[7] Wynkoop, *A Theology of Love*, p. 6.

[8] Chilcote, *Recapturing the Wesleys' Vision*, p 70. This reflection by Wesley was
influenced by Jeremy Taylor, *The Rule and Exercises of Holy Living* (London: F.
Heptinstall, 19th edn, 1703).

led him quickly into love. 'God is love.' Every aspect of the atonement is an expression of love; holiness is love; the meaning of 'religion' is love. Christian perfection is perfection of love. Every step of God toward man, and man's response, step by step, is some aspect of love. Faith works by love. Ethics is the out flowing of love. To say that Christian holiness is our raison d'être (reason to be) is to say we are committed to everything love is, and that is a large order indeed. It is impossible to extract a doctrine of holiness out of Wesley and suppose that love may be discarded with impunity. Christian perfection, cut off from the aorta of all that love is, becomes sterile, cold, dead, incredible.[9]

Therefore, Wesley felt strongly that the key is in humanity relating with God. Moral image flows relationally from breathing in and breathing out God's life, a spiritual respiration. In this way, we mirror the Creator. Wesley saw new birth as needed to bring participation in and partnership with the divine Spirit. In the same way, sanctification is participation in the divine nature (2 Pet 1.4), participation in the mind of Christ (Phil 2.5), or the renewal of the heart after the image of Christ (Col 3.10). Therefore, sanctification restores to fallen humanity that existence in fellowship with the Creator and life as a faithful steward of all that is made.[10]

Consider these biblical texts pointing to humanity's fellowship with God:

And remember, I am with you always, to the end of the age (Mt. 28.20b NRSV).

Even the mystery which hath been hid from ages and from generations, but now is made manifest to his saints: To whom God would make known what is the riches of the glory of this mystery among the Gentiles; which is Christ in you, the hope of glory: Whom we preach, warning every man, and teaching every man in all wisdom; that we may present every man perfect in Christ Jesus: Whereunto I also labor, striving according to his working, which works in me mightily (Col. 1.26-29).

---

[9] Wynkoop, *A Theology of Love*, p. 21.
[10] Runyon, *The New Creation: John Wesley's Theology Today*, pp 14, 18, 19, 22, 82.

What agreement is there between the temple of God and idols? for we are the temple of the living God. As God has said: I will live with them and walk among them, and I will be their God, and they will be my people. Therefore come out from them and be separate, says the Lord. Touch no unclean thing, and I will receive you. I will be a Father to you, and you will be my sons and daughters, says the Lord Almighty (2 Cor. 6.16-18 NIV).

In this new relational mode, Wesley explained that experiential knowledge of God makes one a participant with God as the Eastern Fathers believed. So grace could no longer be defined as a metaphysical gift independent of consciousness, such as election; but grace now became a conscious encounter with God through Christ by the Holy Spirit to the hearts of human beings. Wesley was attacked for teaching this 'perceptible inspiration'. But he pointed to Article 17 of the Anglican 39 Articles, which states that godly person's feel in themselves the working of the Spirit of Christ.[11] Wesley believed that at 'every point the relation between God and man is a fully personal one. By this it is meant that salvation does not occur in any of its phases on sub-rational, nonmoral, substance levels (either corporeal or non-corporeal) of human existence'.[12] This personal fellowship and partnership understanding was not a common understanding or experience of Wesley's day.[13]

It was quite a departure from the norm for Wesley to center his theology on love. He felt strongly that love

in the biblical and Hebraic sense is the deepest motivational focus of personality. It is that centering, organizing principle which gives direction to life. It is everything the person is and does to find personal fulfillment. It is the dynamic of the personality. It is perhaps the only truly free thing about man. It cannot be coerced.[14]

For Wesley, it was the love of God that was seeking and reaching for lost humanity. Wesley described this love as 'prevenient grace',

---

[11] Runyon, *The New Creation: John Wesley's Theology Today*, pp 150-51.

[12] Wynkoop, *A Theology of Love*, p. 64.

[13] Adewuya, *Holiness in the Letters of Paul*, insists that 'holiness demands a divine-human partnership … It is not automatic,' p. 162.

[14] Wynkoop, *A Theology of Love*, p. 64.

God at work in the world constantly influencing and drawing lost humankind to himself. Prevenient grace is the grace that comes before any conscious personal experience of divine grace. This means the first move is God's. Without prevenient grace it is impossible for humans to come to God on their own.[15] For Wesley, the 'prevenient grace' of God was a much better description of the biblical God of love, always moving toward the lost, over against the popular description of his day, a sovereign God who had decreed this metaphysical gift independent of consciousness. That was far too cold and impersonal for him. Wesley saw love as the foundation and therefore relation was the grand vehicle, God relating with humanity, even before humanity could be aware. Prevenient grace leads us to God by creating our first sensitivity to God, giving us a transient conviction, and activating our first wish to please God. So prevenient grace gives us 'response-ability'.[16] Like the Eastern Fathers, Wesley preferred a description of salvation that was relational and where God invited humanity to know him and to participate in partnership with him.

At times Wesley called the relating between God and humanity intercourse, highlighting its relational and intimate nature. M.B. Wynkoop describes this, saying,

> Man must approach the rendezvous with God with the totality of his being. He must contribute something to the interchange. He cannot know without giving himself. This is the meaning of intercourse. It mirrors the Old Testament expression 'to know' someone. [*yada*] In this 'knowing' the most real kind of 'dialogue' is experienced.[17]

She continues,

> One need only pick up and read at random any of Wesley's works to become aware of the thoroughly personal relationship which he presupposes between God and man. This is quite different from theologies which stress first the absolute sovereignty of God to the loss of the possibility of true dialogue. With Wesley, God is seeking man, creating situations to get his attention,

---

[15] Harper, *The Way to Heaven*, p. 34.
[16] Harper, *The Way to Heaven*, pp. 35, 37.
[17] Wynkoop, *A Theology of Love*, p. 66.

appealing to him, cajoling him, wanting his love, and expecting his freely given fellowship.[18]

To know God, to 'be saved', is to love Him – and love is the most personal thing in the world. In fact it could be said that what one loves is what one is. Love is self-giving and receiving. It is the totality, of the self finding itself in the totality of another. It is not a state but a movement, a relationship; it is not a quantity but a quality; it is not a law but a life. In his Notes, Wesley said, 'We love him because he first loved us' – [I John 4.19]. This is the sum of all religion, the genuine model of Christianity. None can say more. Why should anyone say less? or less intelligibly?"[19]

Wesley's fundamental point of view, the characteristic which made it identifiable from other points of view, is the conviction that man's relationship to God and God's relation to man is a personal relationship and that all facets of theology and life partake of this personal nature and must be interpreted in this light. He felt that this way of thinking was biblical and did justice to what he knew about human nature and total personal experience – his own and others.[20]

Wesley's love center and relational foundation naturally led to his consecration model, which was so radical to his generation. The consecration model will be discussed fully in Chapter 4. Yet, in this chapter it should be noted that Wesley's consecration model flows directly out of his love center and relational foundation. Consider this in the light of the previous quote, '… sanctification restores to fallen man that existence in fellowship with the Creator and life'.[21] Given this restoration of relating, then it would be logical to understand that securing, maintaining, and augmenting this relationship, this fellowship, would be the most critical work of the Church toward believers. Wesley held this perception and motivated his people in consecration flowing from the heart toward further and further relational experience with God.

---

[18] Wynkoop, *A Theology of Love*, p. 66.
[19] Wynkoop, *A Theology of Love*, p. 67.
[20] Wynkoop, *A Theology of Love*, p. 75.
[21] Theodore Runyon, *The New Creation*, pp. 14, 18, 19, 22, 82.

Wesley's vision was of love for God motivating greater and greater personal experience with God (fellowship), which would result in continuing growth in sanctification and holiness. This vision can be seen in Paul's words to the Corinthians, 'But we all, with open face beholding as in a glass the glory of the Lord, are changed into the same image from glory to glory, *even* as by the Spirit of the Lord' (2 Cor. 3.18). This is why leading believers into continued and deeper depths of relating with God was such a crucial element in Wesley's vision for holiness by sanctification.

It can be said that this was radical to Wesley's day because the Church had become cold and greatly institutional. Personal experience of God had not been greatly encouraged in the Reformation; and now, two hundred years later, that level of spirituality was missing generally. We even see from comments Wesley makes in his journals that his mother Susanna walked through the vast majority of her life in the Church without giving testimony to personal experience with God. If that be true of Susanna, a woman of great conviction and life commitment, the general state of the Church was certainly far below this.[22]

Love-Based

Mary Tooth, a Wesleyan and leader in the movement, said, 'If you get your heart full of the love of God, you will find that is the oil by which the lamp of faith will be ever kept burning'.[23]

As a remarkable Biblical scholar, Wesley founded his teaching of sanctification on the most central command of scripture, the Great Commandment!

> [35] One of them, an expert in the law, tested him with this question: [36] Teacher, which is the greatest commandment in the Law? [37] Jesus replied: Love the Lord your God with all your heart and with all your soul and with all your mind. [38] This is the first and greatest commandment. [39] And the second is like it: Love your neighbor as yourself. [40] All the Law and the Prophets hang on these two commandments (Mt. 22.35-40 NIV).

---

[22] Collins, *John Wesley: A Theological Journey*, pp. 119-20.
[23] Chilcote, *Recapturing the Wesleys' Vision*, p. 74.

Of course, Wesley knew that he had chosen the most solid foundation possible for sanctification, perfect love. A simple search for scriptures using both words, love and perfect, brings impressive results. See, for example, the following:

He that dwells in love, dwells in God, and God in him. Herein is our love made perfect ... (1 Jn 4.16-17).

If we love one another, God dwells in us, and his love is perfected in us (1 Jn 4.12).

And above all these things, put on charity which is the bond of perfectness (Col. 3.14).

Now the end (*telos*) of the commandment is charity, out of a pure heart, and of a good conscience (1 Tim. 1.5).

And now abides faith, hope, charity, these three, but the greatest of these is charity (1 Cor 13.12).

Methodism was deeply rooted in the piety of the heart, creating a spirituality that was more Catholic than Protestant, based on love of God rather than faith in Christ.[24] Holiness in the first stage is cleansing, but that is the least and lowest branch, the negative part of our salvation. The positive part is 'that we may love thee'. And, in reality, the fulfillment of the positive serves to answer the negative as well. If love fills the whole heart, where is there room for sin?[25] So for Wesley, true Christianity was holiness of heart and life, and he concluded that inward holiness consisted of perfect love, which is expressed outwardly in holy living.[26]

This holy love grants the mind of Christ (Phil. 2.5), bears the fruit of the Spirit (Gal. 5.22-23), renews the image of God (Eph. 4.24), issues forth in inward and outward holiness (1 Pet. 1.15), and offers itself sacrificially (Mt. 1.21). Those who are crucified with Christ manifest love in all kinds of situations with every attitude and act (Gal. 2.20). Indeed, as Wesley says, 'Faith working by love is the length and breadth and depth and height of Christian perfection' (See Eph. 5.6).

---

[24] Chilcote, *Recapturing the Wesleys' Vision*, pp. 73-74.
[25] Runyon, *The New Creation: John Wesley's Theology Today*, p. 85.
[26] Knight III, *From Aldersgate to Azusa Street*, p. 17.

Head and Heart

Because love was the foundation of Wesley's teaching, the heart then replaced the head as the center of attention. In the tradition of Kempis, Taylor, and Law, Wesley stressed simplicity of intention or purity of affection. In his view of inward faith, dispositions of the heart were central. His faith was not mind centered or based on intellectual assent. He believed that through the dispositions of the heart, a transformation of being, a modification of life would take place by the presence of the Holy Spirit that makes believers holy and thereby empowers them for obedience, the very heart of gospel liberty.[27] Therefore, consuming love brings liberty from the dominion of sin. In Wesley's sermon, The Scripture Way of Salvation', Wesley describes entire sanctification as 'love excluding sin, love filling the heart, love taking up the whole capacity of the soul … For as long as love takes up the whole heart, what room is there for sin therein?'[28]

Wesley appreciated the foundation of faith that came from the Reformation, but he taught that love was the best center piece for the way of salvation and the Christian life. According to Wesley, too much emphasis on justification by faith caused believers to feel the work was all done right there in the justification/regeneration act.[29] (Has anyone ever seen a believer that was saved and satisfied to sit?) Wesley felt that love for God would continue to move believers onward into his presence by the means of grace to become more and more like him through the sanctifying work, both crisis and process. One of Wesley's favorite scriptures was Gal. 5.6 that says 'faith works by love'. For Wesley, love built faith into assuring trust and love motivated works of piety and mercy. He felt love was the better

---

[27] Collins, *John Wesley: A Theological Journey*, p. 145.
[28] Wesley, 'The Scripture Way of Salvation', as quoted in Greathouse, *Love Made Perfect: Foundations for the Holy Life*, p. 46.
[29] Runyon, *The New Creation: John Wesley's Theology Today*, p. 49. See also p. 53. Wesley saw the work of justification not as a transaction but as a means to communicate the love of God, relational rather than judicial. Wesley moved from faith as assent to faith as trust which involves relationship (p. 54). Later but in a similar vein, Martin Buber said faith is the response called out by the Thou and continuing relationship empowered by the Thou (p. 54). Wesley would not appreciate conversion decisions since they lack the direction of the continuing work of the Spirit toward the goal of the image of God. He called it a tragic misunderstanding of salvation by faith (p. 58).

foundation (consequently, Jesus called love 'the great commandment').

We know that one may hold orthodox beliefs and yet not have saving grace. Wesley insisted on the priority of orthopraxy over orthodoxy in faith, a lived faith. But works are of no value unless God is the covenant partner and producer of our works in a continuing synergistic relationship. Humans cannot produce this alone. Therefore, orthodoxy is not the answer and orthopraxy by itself is insufficient. Orthopathy supplies the needed element, the new sensitivity to and participation in spiritual reality that mark's genuine faith.[30] Wesley chose right passions (orthopathy) as the cornerstone of faith, which would motivate right practice (orthopraxy), and would activate right belief (orthodoxy), the latter two tended to be stagnant and stale on their own.[31]

Listen to Wesley speak about love and the heart, the relational key of holiness:

> Love is the end of every commandment of God. It is the point aimed at by the whole and every part of the Christian institution. The foundation is faith, purifying the heart, the end love, preserving the conscience[32] ... Love is the fulfilling of the law, the end of the commandment. It is not only the first and great commandment, but all the commandments in one. The royal law of heaven and earth is this, Thou shalt love the Lord thy God with all thy heart, and with all thy soul, and mind and strength. I concluded in these words: Here is the sum of the perfect law, the circumcision of the heart. It may be observed, this sermon was composed the first of all my writings which have been published. This was the view of religion I had then, which even then I scrupled not to term perfection. This is the view I have of it now, without any material addition or diminution.[33]

Wesley states further,

---

[30] Runyon, *The New Creation: John Wesley's Theology Today*, pp. 147-149.

[31] Land, *Pentecostal Spirituality*, pp. 41-46. Land speaks of the interaction between beliefs, actions, and affections and provides a broad discussion for this synthesis.

[32] John Wesley, *Works of the Rev. John Wesley*, XI, p. 416, as quoted in Wynkoop, p. 8.

[33] Wesley, *Works of the Rev. John Wesley*, XI, pp. 367-68, as quoted in Wynkoop, p. 8-9.

It were well you should be thoroughly sensible of this, The heaven of heavens is love. There is nothing higher in religion; there is, in effect, nothing else; if you look for anything more than love, you are looking wide of the mark, you are getting out of the royal way, and when you are asking others, Have you received this or that blessing? if you mean anything but more love, you mean wrong; you are leading them out of the way, and putting them upon a false scent. Settle it then in your heart, that from the moment God has saved you from all sin, you are to aim at nothing more, but more of that love described in the thirteenth of the Corinthians. You can go no higher than this, till you are carried into Abraham's bosom?[34]

Legalism

It seems appropriate to conclude this chapter by talking some about the perversion of love-centered holiness which so thoroughly overtook the Holiness movement and continued as well in the Holiness Pentecostal movements of the early 1900's. The perversion was legalism, measuring holiness by the criteria of outward behaviors. Naturally this development led to a de-emphasis on growth in holiness through inner spiritual experience by relating with God, the love center of holiness/sanctification.

William Greathouse says, 'From the beginning covenant love has been the essence of holiness: human love responding in radical obedience to God's redeeming love. To miss this truth inevitably leads to loveless legalism.'[35]

Roberta Bondi has studied the early monastic fathers and gives their perspective. In the fourth century, with the Desert Fathers and the beginning of monasticism, what called so many away from ordinary life and into the desert was the commandment, 'Be ye perfect, as your heavenly Father is perfect' (Mt. 5.48). Though it is strange from our modern point of view, this commandment did not seem repulsive or impossible to them. Today it suggests legalism or

---

[34] Wesley, *Works of the Rev. John Wesley*, XI, p. 430, as quoted in Wynkoop, p. 14.

[35] Greathouse, *Love Made Perfect*, p. 44.

it fills hearts with despair. But 'for those Desert Fathers the command to be perfect was simply another way of stating the Great Commandment, loving God and others fully. They believed this is what Jesus asked of those that took up his life, perfect love.'[36]

Pastor Steve Spears joins the conversation on legalism and holy living:

> In the past we quickly moved from a Spirit-oriented sanctification to a rules oriented sanctification. This has often looked like the right way, but never could bring us to the goal (Col. 2.21-23). Moreover, even the most holy law was powerless to save and sanctify (Rom. 8.3; Gal. 3.21b) and very hard to bear (Acts 15.10). Our rules have failed us.
>
> Today, there are many wanting to live a more 'authentic' life by eliminating rules and laws. They feel it is being more honest to admit our brokenness and in some sense celebrate such brokenness. This is a flawed attempt to elevate the amazing gift of grace. Now we do want to be honest. We are all broken (most of us severely). But that is the point. Jesus offers (in Wesley's words) the double cure. Grace is the power to overcome, not the celebration of sin. It would seem we have stumbled so much that many have given up. Jesus' work on the cross and the gift of the Holy Spirit offers us so much more. Our quest for authenticity has failed us as well.
>
> Where I believe the Lord is leading us is to build Spirit-instilled character that can withstand the temptations of youth and adulthood. Character that is not based strictly on rules, but on a life so filled and in tune with the Spirit that the standard of holiness goes beyond rule following and is what some call 'second nature' – it just happens as a result of a transformed, disciplined life. Yet, it does not 'just happen'. It takes effort to build such character – perhaps 'being intentional' – better communicates this.
>
> Rules are given to curb our first (fallen) nature. We are called to develop 'second natures' that are undergirded and empowered by the Spirit not law. I want to ask, can we eliminate (or better

---

[36] Roberta C. Bondi, *To Love as God Loves* (Philadelphia, PA: Fortress Press, 1987), p 20.

set to the side) our rules and see what life in the Spirit will produce? Can we trust the gift from the Father to be the answer we need? Can we trust that the power of the Spirit is enough to move us toward our goal?[37]

Pastor Spears touches some key issues as we reflect on the perversion to love-centered holiness which has been so prominent in our past. Pastor Spear's emphasis on the Spirit for holiness will be discussed in Chapter 6, but it reminds me of Paul declaring that 'God's love has been poured out into our hearts by the Holy Spirit which has been given to us' (Rom. 5.5 NRSV).

Wynkoop said,

Love takes the Harshness out of Holiness. Love takes the Incredibility out of Perfection. Love takes the Antinomianism out of Faith. Love takes the Moralism out of Obedience. Love takes the Gnosticism out of Cleansing. Love takes the Abstraction out of Truth. Love puts the Personal into Truth. Love puts the Ethical into Holiness. Love puts Process into Life. Love puts Urgency into Crisis. Love puts Seriousness into Sin. Love puts Fellowship into Perfection.[38]

Wesley's own words strike a blow against legalism:

This religion we long to see established in the world, a religion of love, and joy, and peace, having its seat in the inmost soul, but ever showing itself by its fruits, continually springing forth, not only in all innocence (for love worketh no ill to his neighbor), but likewise in every beneficence, spreading virtue and happiness all around it.[39]

Legalism is often motivated by fear rather than by love. Wesley is known for his description of four kinds of Christians and how they are involved in fear or love: the natural man, with neither fear

---

[37] Steve Spears, 'Legalism and Holy Living', article shared in personal correspondence in dialogue about the need for renewal in the holiness/sanctification message, August 2015. Pastor Spears ministers in Collinsville, AL.

[38] Wynkoop, *A Theology of Love*, p. 8.

[39] John Wesley, 'An Earnest Appeal to Men of Reason and Religion, London: Wesleyan Conference Office', in *Works of the Rev. John Wesley*, XIV, p. 4, as quoted in Wynkoop, *A Theology of Love*, p 9. Could there be a better description of the impact that John Wesley's Methodist movement had on the nation of England?

nor love; the awakened man, with fear and no love; a babe in Christ with fear and love; and a father in Christ who has love without fear.[40] The exchange between fear and love has often played a great role in how legalism flourished. Ziefle says, 'Separation has been the classic response to fear-based ministry motivation with the set apart meaning of holiness being emphasized there. So, the image is retreat from the world. This can lead to either legalism or elitism, or both'.[41]

Sin has also been a central topic in the legalism conversation. Most often legalism described sin as acts to be committed. But Wesley took it deeper than this and spoke of sin in relational terms. His classic definition is that sin is 'every voluntary breach of the law of love'.[42] At sin's base, Wesley described sin as broken relationship, whether that brokenness is expressed toward others or toward God. And it is important to note that breach is conscious and willful. For Wesley, sin is not something that sneaks up on you; it arises out of you.[43]

The 'disposition of the heart' was a cornerstone phrase for Wesley in the context of holiness as relation and love. At the heart of Christian holiness was 'singleness of intention'. This can be found in the will, not in one's actions. Actions can vary, while intentions can remain constant. This does not minimize actions, but it does mean that the experience of being is deeper than the level of doing. It means a believer has discovered a 'central purpose of life' – a purpose that gives meaning, direction, and power to life. For Wesley, this purpose was The Great Commandment (Mt. 22.37-39). 'Wesley saw (as did many before him) that the primary intention, the "controlling desire," is our resolve to love God and others'.[44]

A 'disposition of the heart' is a deep attitude of heart that flows from love based in commitment. This kind of love is not characterized by emotion, though emotion certainly must be a part of such

---

[40] Greathouse, *Love Made Perfect*, p. 106.

[41] Joshua Ziefle, 'From Fear-Based to Holiness-Based: Thoughts About the Work of the Holy Spirit in Youth Ministry', in Lee Roy Martin (ed.), *A Future for Holiness: Pentecostal Explorations* (Cleveland, TN: CPT Press, 2013), p 336.

[42] John Wesley, *The Letters of John Wesley* (ed. J. Telford; London: Epworth, 1931), VI, p. 322.

[43] Wesley, *The Letters of John Wesley*, VI, p. 322, as quoted in Steve Harper, *The Way to Heaven* (Grand Rapids, MI: Zondervan, 2003), p. 23.

[44] Harper, *The Way to Heaven*, p. 84.

love. It is this love of commitment that shapes the way we see, understand, and act. Even when emotion is absent or contrary, this love as a disposition of the heart enables appropriate loving attitudes and actions. Often when we act out of such love, the actual experience feels much more like what we would ordinarily think of as duty. For this reason, choosing this kind of love is a synergistic act that requires the partnership of heavenly grace.[45]

The use of perfection in the Bible and with Wesley is so often misunderstood and offensive to some, but it is held in this concept of the 'disposition of the heart'. Here Christian perfection can be seen as perfection in God's eyes while being flawed as well. Consider the mother who is being offered fresh flowers from her four-year old son. She knows they came from her flower garden in which she has invested so much time and effort to plant. Yet she sees beyond this flaw to the intention of the heart, her son bringing a gift for his mother. She sees perfection of intent while she understands the flawed element.[46]

Isn't it the same for God? In the light of his complete holiness, Isaiah says, 'our righteousnesses are like filthy rags' (Isa. 64.6). Yet God sees the 'disposition of the soul' and understands that our motive, our controlling desire, is to please him and emulate him. It seems this aligns with the teaching of Jesus who talked about life actions flowing 'out of the abundance of the heart' (Mt. 12.34-35). In the same line of thought, Roberta Bondi saw from her study of the fourth-century Fathers that 'the goal of the Christian life has to do with love, not rules. The very purpose of the incarnation was to show the way back to the original image of God in which we were created and enabled to become really loving, truly human'.[47]

Applications

Amazingly the new packaging for a renewal in holiness and sanctification today is the old wrapping that the Holiness movement drifted from in favor of legalism. It is LOVE! This new/old wrapping is the most potent force in the Bible, the Love of God! And

---

[45] Bondi, *To Love as God Loves*, pp. 30, 34.
[46] Harper, *The Way to Heaven*, p. 84.
[47] Bondi, *To Love as God Loves*, p. 21.

by the way, it happens to be one of the most attractive elements for postmoderns, millennials, gen-Xers, ethnic groups, youth, married people, singles, seniors, women, men, poverty stricken, rich, disenfranchised, powerful, educated, illiterate … Ok, you get the message, 'Love Works!'

If having an ongoing relationship with Christ is such a critical key to the sanctifying/transformational process, then aiding believers to develop this relationship must be equally as critical. Wesley saw the 'means of grace' as the way to accomplish this and this volume will touch those in another segment to come (See Chapter 4).

In this relational segment, as mentioned in the motivational segment, the way salvation is described to new converts and believers is of utmost importance. If it is a forensic act, or a once-for-all step taken, then no foundation has been laid to enter and develop a relationship with Christ. In Pentecostalism, we may do the same with the baptism of the Holy Spirit. Neither justification nor Spirit baptism should be a climactic experience to be attained, but they should be entrances into a new and rich life walking with Christ through the Holy Spirit intimately and daily.

Not only should ministry leaders help believers and new converts as they step into salvation and Spirit baptism, but ministry structures need to be in place to help believers to grow in their developing relationship with Christ by the Spirit, to express their sentiments in these growth moments, and to give ongoing encouragement to 'press on toward the mark for the prize'. In a later segment we will talk about the structures Wesley designed and used so effectively. Those may not be the answer for our current challenges for holiness and sanctification, but the principles upon which they are founded will be helpful in guiding the design of new ministry structures (See Chapter 4).

In sanctification, it seems paramount that the believer learn to understand what it means for 'God to work in him, both to will and to do of his good pleasure' (Phil. 2.12). So this relational walk goes beyond Christ who is with us, to an understanding and expectation that Christ is daily working in us to guide, inspire, and empower acts that accomplish 'His good pleasure'. A believer's understanding of and experience walking in the Holy Spirit is paramount here, Christ working in us (See Chapter 6).

Ministers should give thoughtful consideration to making 'Love' the highest achievement of spiritual life and church life. That might mean asking what holds that place now? And how can we shift to a 'Love' criteria in every aspect of spiritual life and church life? How can church life affirm 'loving God and loving others' in practical ways week in and week out? There is a leadership maxim that says, 'What gets affirmed, gets done'. Love must take the highest place in our hierarchy of priority spiritually and in ministry.

Important progress should be made in shifting matters of faith (that is, the major life-consuming work of sanctification and holiness) from focus on the intellect, head, to a focus on the passions, heart. From the reformation and the Enlightenment, spiritual matters have been dominated by the intellect, but Wesley gives us a taste of faith from a new center, orthopathy, the passions. Today is the day for this shift, if not late, since postmodernism brings a receptivity to this new foundation in the passions. Also, Pentecost is greatly compatible with such a shift. Implications of this should include looking at Wesley's methods as well as creating new methods to make this shift in every aspect of faith expression.[48] As we are learning, orthodoxy cannot stand without orthopraxy, and orthopraxy is highly improbable without orthopathy. This shift is a must and long overdue. Wesley can help us get the ball rolling in this day.

Today, more than at any other time, legalism must be rejected in all of its forms. Wesley's approach can help greatly in this as salvation is proclaimed and experienced as a relationship with Christ where love is the central element, the Spirit is shown to pour out this love in believers, and the goal of all Christian life is the fullness of holy love.

---

[48] Consider, as one area to be examined, Cheryl Bridges Johns' work in a new approach to Bible study that incorporates far more than information transfer. See her work, *Pentecostal Formation: A Pedagogy among the Oppressed* (JPTSup 2; Sheffield, UK: Sheffield Academic Press, 1993), pp. 130-37. See also James K.A. Smith, *Desiring the Kingdom* (Grand Rapids, MI: Baker Academics, 2009), where Smith describes faith approaches that release faith from the intellect/head/information mode, accenting body involvement as well.

John Wesley's Prayer

O my God, fill my soul with so entire a love of You, that I may love nothing but for your sake, subordinating every-thing else to You.

Give me grace so to study Your knowledge daily that the more I know You the more I love You.

Create in me a zealous obedience to Your commands, a cheerful patience under chastisements, and a thankful resig-nation in my losses.

May I always have awesome thoughts of You, never men-tioning Your venerable Name except on solemn and devout occasions, and not even then without acts of adoration.

O make the one business of my life to glorify You by every thought of my heart, every word of my tongue, every work of my hands. Help me to do this by professing Your truth even to death, if that would please You. More, help me en-gage all people, so far as in me lies, to glorify and love You. Amen.[49]

---

[49] Wesley, *Wesley's Daily Prayers*, p. 448.

3

TRANSFORMATION

We know of no gospel without salvation from sin.[1]   – John Wesley

The testimony of some historians that the Wesleyan revival was the greatest force for social change in the eighteenth century is a testimony to the legitimacy of Christian methods to evoke transformation.[2]
                                                                    – Steve Harper

When on the individual level Christian perfection becomes the goal, a fundamental hope is aroused that the future can surpass the present. And a corresponding holy dissatisfaction is aroused with regard to any present state of affairs, a dissatisfaction that supplies the critical edge necessary to keep the process of individual transformation moving.[3]
                                                                    – Theodore Runyon

Transformation Power

It is highly likely that the change that takes place in a life through salvation is the most powerful witness to the validity and authority of the Christian gospel. History affirms that the Wesleyan movement produced this kind of transforming change in lives by the thousands all across England and then transported such a gospel to

---

[1] Wesley, *The Letters of John Wesley*, VI, p. 327, as quoted in Steve Harper, *The Way to Heaven: The Gospel According to John Wesley* (Grand Rapids: Zondervan, 2003), p. 23.

[2] Harper, *The Way to Heaven*, p. 138.

[3] Runyon, *The New Creation*, p. 168.

the newly-formed United States. The central thesis of this volume is that *Words from Wesley* on core themes of the Wesleyan movement, such as life transforming power in the gospel message, are needed today. Observations, surveys, polls, and studies continue to show that there is little significant difference between believers and non-believers in a wide range of life behaviors today.[4] The Christian kingdom in the West particularly has all but lost this validity and the authority of the Christian gospel. This chapter considers Wesley's view and commitment to transformation of life under the influence of the grace of God, whether at conversion, or especially through the gracious full-life process of sanctification. Wesley's ministry embraced the ontological reality of Paul's words to the Corinthians, 'Therefore if any man be in Christ he is a new creature. Old things are passed away, behold all things are become new' (2 Cor. 5.17).

Notably, Terry Johns writes,

> Transformed affections are the core of our new identity. Real change is represented – genuine transformation that is ontological in nature. With the transformation of affections a change of being takes place. We do not simply identify with God, but are transformed to the very presence of God, and participate, through the Holy Spirit, in the life of God. Every relationship is affected and our way of being in the world is repositioned. That is, our transformed nature results in a new expression of life and values.[5]

Wesley's world was filled with desperation. People by the masses were reaching for something that would lift their lives up and out of dire circumstance where disaster seemed imminent daily.[6] It was Wesley, whom God used to see their need and discern how to bring the Gospel solution to them in a way that could reach them and could genuinely transform their lives. In the business world it is

---

[4] Barna Group, 'The Concept of Holiness Baffles Most Christians', online article, accessed May 15, 2015, https://www.barna.org/barna-update/5-barna-update/162-the-concept-of-holiness-baffles-most-americans#.VS1g3_nF-ik.

[5] Terry Johns, 'The Practice of Holiness: Implications for a Pentecostal Moral Theology', in Lee Roy Martin (ed.), *A Future for Holiness: Pentecostal Explorations* (Cleveland, TN: CPT Press, 2013), p. 306.

[6] Knight III, *From Aldersgate to Azusa Street*, p. 136.

possible to see a solution but to find no avenue to deliver the product to the very ones that need it. The Spirit of God prepared Wesley for just such a task, and the transformation of England was the result.

It may be significant for us in the context of this volume to note that the Great Awakening of England came at a time when the Church of England was weak in her spiritual expression and influence nationally.[7] Yet we can see that God was preparing ministry that would rise up and bring a radical renewal to the land. Believers must never give up on their hope, or confidence, that God is at work to revive what seems quite dead. On the other hand believers must recognize that God is not limited and may choose to work outside the norms of the established church structure when he can find no other source for his awakening call. If we believe the Church in our culture is at great loss today for the lack of holiness, 1) we must not give up hope, and 2) we must anticipate God's answer to come from any direction he might choose. Consider Wesley, who was used by God to bring transformation to millions of lives, whose ministry was perceived to come from outside the structure of the Church of England, whose influence for change was felt in both England and the new United States – whose example for renewal in holiness remains as the mark for which generations have striven.

Grace Brings Change

One of the most distinctive characteristics of Wesleyan Christianity was the emphasis on the salvation 'process' to make a real change in a life. 'To put it simply, if your faith as a Christian is genuine, then other people will be able to see it lived out in loving ways. Faith in Jesus Christ is not real until it is connected to how you live day to day.'[8] That change can be described as dealing with negative aspects, such as evil and sin, or it can be described as dealing with positive aspects, such as dispositions of the heart, fruit of the Spirit, and

---

[7] Albert C. Outler, *John Wesley* (New York: Oxford, 1964, 1980), p. 386. Wesley said, 'We see on every side either men of no religion at all, or men of a lifeless, formal religion. We are grieved at the sight.'

[8] Chilcote, *Recapturing the Wesleys' Vision*, p. 25.

holy love. But for Wesley there could never be satisfaction with any teaching about salvation that left a person in the same state, the same behavior patterns, the same evil that had been present previously.

The Old Testament prophets spoke of this newness of life:

> This is the covenant I will make with the house of Israel after that time, declares the LORD. I will put my law in their minds and write it on their hearts. I will be their God, and they will be my people (Jer. 31.33 NIV).

> Then will I sprinkle clean water upon you, and ye shall be clean: from all your filthiness, and from all your idols, will I cleanse you. [26] A new heart also will I give you, and a new spirit will I put within you: and I will take away the stony heart out of your flesh, and I will give you an heart of flesh. [27] And I will put my spirit within you, and cause you to walk in my statutes, and ye shall keep my judgments, and do them (Ezek. 36.25-27).

Ezekiel speaks of a 'divine heart transplant', where God promises to remove the heart of stone and give us a tender obedient heart of flesh that is filled with the Spirit to empower us to walk in his statutes and keep his judgments. 'What Ezekiel's promise means experientially is that the disposition of inordinate self love that is our inheritance as members of Adam's fallen race will be displaced by that "habitual disposition of the soul" which in the sacred writings is termed holiness'.[9] What many today feel is to be a 'super Christian', Wesley felt was simply the call to be a normal Christian.[10] Hollis Gause agreed with Wesley saying, 'The pursuit of holiness is the normal manner of life for the believer'.[11] This life is characterized by the pursuit of freedom from sinning, by the denial of the lust of the flesh, the lust of the eye and the pride of life, and by a cultivation of the fruit of the Spirit. In the context of this chapter continuing change is expected and ongoing.

---

[9] Greathouse, *Love Made Perfect*, p. 49.

[10] Greathouse, *Love Made Perfect*, p. 59. The term 'habitual disposition of the soul' is drawn from John Wesley's sermon 'Circumcision of the Heart', found in John Wesley, *The Works of John Wesley* (ed. Thomas Jackson; Grand Rapids: Baker Books, 1979), I, p. 267.

[11] Hollis Gause, *Living in the Spirit: The Way of Salvation* (Cleveland, TN: Pathway Press, 1980), p. 12.

Wesley wanted to hold the cross and the resurrection together – the price paid and the power given, inward then outward. Wesley certainly appreciated the work of justification by faith. He saw justification as what Christ does 'for us', delivering us from the guilt of sin. But the passion of Wesley's life was sanctification, God working 'in us' to deliver us from the power of sin. In justification the price was paid and peace of soul is given. And in sanctification, grace gives us the power to be free from the dominion of sin and the power to love God fully and to love others graciously. In these two, Wesley opposed the antinomian implication that we can remain sinners while Christ's righteousness covers us, holding the cross and the resurrection together - the price paid and the power given.[12]

Wesley spoke about being saved from the power of sin as well as the guilt of sin. 'None that is not saved from sin here can be saved from hell hereafter'.[13] It took Wesley considerable time in his life and ministry to work out the proper distinctions of God's grace. He taught that a justified person is freed from the guilt of sin; a regenerated person is freed from sin's power; and the entirely sanctified person is freed from sin's being.[14] In the same vein, William Greathouse recalled Gustaf Aulen's classic work, *Christus Victor*, saying, 'Christ died and rose, not to cover up sin, but to destroy it'.[15] This generation seems to want justification to be a blanket coverage for all our sins, past, present, and future. (This idea does seem to encourage antinomianism on some level.) But Wesley saw grace, especially in regeneration and sanctification, as breaking the power of sin so that individuals did not have to live under the bondage of sin any longer. There is quite a difference between these two views.

God's Image Formed

For Wesley, the goal of theology is transformation. On the positive side, in the sanctifying work we have dealt previously with the grace that is active in filling our hearts with holy love. The goal of that

---

[12] Chilcote, *Recapturing the Wesleys' Vision*, pp. 29-31.

[13] John Wesley, 'A Blow at the Root; or, Christ Stabbed in the House of His Friends', in Wesley, *Works of the Rev. John Wesley*, X, p. 364.

[14] Collins, *John Wesley: A Theological Journey*, pp. 96-97.

[15] Greathouse, *Love Made Perfect*, p. 55. See Gustaf Aulen, *Christus Victor* (trans. A.G. Herbert; New York: MacMillan Co., 1951), pp. 16-35.

holy love is that the believer may be formed into the very image of God through the sanctification process. Paul speaks of this process:

> Now the Lord is the Spirit, and where the Spirit of the Lord is, there is freedom. And all of us, with unveiled faces, seeing the glory of the Lord as though reflected in a mirror, are being transformed into the same image from one degree of glory to another; for this comes from the Lord, the Spirit (2 Cor. 3.17-18 NRSV).

This process was Wesley's passion. He emphasized that salvation is not just being reinstated in God's favor, but salvation also aims to restore believers to the image of God. This is the work of sanctification. Wesley was not satisfied with the concept of justification, that God cloaks us in his righteousness. For him, that remained external with little real change taking place in the believer's life. He saw in Holy Scripture that God wants to implant righteousness in us in such a way that it grows touching every aspect of our lives.[16]

Greathouse expounds on the familiar passage, Gal. 2.20, 'I am crucified with Christ, nevertheless I live, yet not I, but Christ lives in me':

> It describes a sinful self to be crucified with Christ, a human self to be disciplined in Christ, and a true self to be actualized in Christ ... In fullest Christian perspective, self fulfillment is only the bi-product of crucifixion with Christ. The end God has in mind in our crucifixion with Christ is actualization of the divine self – 'not I but Christ'. Self-actualization is the ideal of the so-called New Age movement; Christ-actualization is the goal of the gospel.[17]

Greathouse goes on to say, 'God's purpose in crucifying my pretentious self is simply that Christ may become reincarnate in me and live out his life of holy, loving servitude in my every day, humdrum existence'.[18]

---

[16] Runyon, *The New Creation*, pp. 86, 90.
[17] Greathouse, *Love Made Perfect*, p. 64.
[18] Greathouse, *Love Made Perfect*, p. 72.

Via Salutis

In this journey of transformation, it is beneficial for the participants to understand, at least in broad terms, the direction of the journey, the goal, and critical points along the way. Traditionally this language, particularly if applied with dogmatic rigidity, is designated the *ordo salutis*; but, for Wesley/Wesleyans, including Wesleyan-Pentecostals, it is better described as *via salutis*, suggesting more dynamic fluidity. Obviously, the journey starts with prevenient grace drawing us, and moves through repentance/confession to justification and regeneration. At this point, even Wesley is not crystal clear whether initial sanctification was a function of regeneration or would it be a part of an attitude change or perspective change in the believer subsequent to but flowing from regeneration? Here there is room for diversity with Wesley. From regeneration gradual sanctification continues the transforming process as the believer interacts with God through the means of grace and the work of the Spirit. In time, as the believer presses on in growth by grace, the crisis experience of entire sanctification occurs, often deeply perceived but possibly imperceptible to some.[19] From that level of maturity the believer continues to grow in relationship with God who cannot be fully known even through eternity. Always and in each step along this path the direction and goal is to be conformed to the image of God, his holiness, and love. Finally, stepping over from this life, the believer is glorified in the presence of God forever.

From this simple listing of the order of salvation it is obvious that there are crisis moments to be experienced and seasons of gradual growth and maturing as the believer walks toward the image of Christ. Of course, arching over the entirety of this journey is the trajectory of forward motion through steps and stages of transformation. Experience, as well as Bible reading, also gives us the understanding that in addition to the events given here, there can be numerous other moments of crisis experience along this sanctification road. Paul's description from 2 Cor. 3.18 above uses the phrase 'from one degree of glory to another', or the familiar KJV, 'from glory to glory'. These moments of crisis may bring the believer to

---

[19] Cox, *John Wesley's Concept of Perfection*, pp. 88-92, 94-102.

either an advance in the positive aspects of sanctification, adding qualities of the Christ life, or help advancement through laying down negative aspects, dealing with some temptation, evil, or carnal influence that would hinder further progress on the way.

It is likely that modern Christianity has all but lost a sense of the *ordo salutis* that has been held throughout the history of Christian faith and theology, regardless of the various schools of thought. The elements may have been different in different faith streams, but the value of an *ordo salutis* was held in common through history. Could there be a relationship between the loss of clarity about the *ordo salutis* and a loss of passion for advancement in biblical holiness and sanctification?

Crisis and Process

Considering this anticipation of crisis and process as we walk through ongoing transformation, the Bible language used in connection with holiness and sanctification can be descriptive and helpful. 'Crucifixion' and 'mortification' appear to be serious descriptions that draw on death language. 'Living sacrifice' might fit in that category also. 'Circumcision of the heart' from Old Testament language speaks of 'cutting away' fleshly desires. 'Cleansing' and 'washing' are familiar as modes of dealing with unholy entities within. 'Laying aside' paints a picture of some elements that should not be carried further on the holiness path. And Paul uses 'putting off' and 'putting on' in a similar way, teaching the Colossian and Ephesian saints how to grow in Christlikeness. The positive descriptions are helpful also, such as Christ's teaching on perfection (Mt. 5.48) and Peter's on being holy (1 Pet. 1.15-16). Aspiring to the 'mind of Christ' and the 'renewal of the mind' sheds light on facets to be sought in sanctification's continuing development. 'Follow Christ's steps' would be one illustration of the admonitions to imitate our Lord in life. And of course, Jesus' teaching in the Great Commandment, loving God and loving others, is the prototype for Wesley in all sanctification development.

Wesley at times 'described the movement toward God in metaphorical terms of gestation (prevenient grace), birth (justifying grace), and death (sanctifying grace)'.[20] Many appreciate the use of death in this metaphor to illustrate sanctification. There is a feeling that 'humanism' has made such strong inroads into western thinking that today it is politically incorrect, or would that be evangelically incorrect, to speak of death, or crucifixion, or mortification of the self flesh man, or the carnal man, or the old man. Though Christ went to the cross and died for us, the forces resisting our death for him are imposing today. This points back to a total loss of the doctrine, or understanding at the grass roots, of the corruption from the Fall as well as the finished work system's total reliance on God's sovereign decree so that there is no further need to mortify oneself. Again, humanism permeating our culture in diverse forms has influenced the spiritual thought of believers. Paul was not hesitant to say, 'I am crucified with Christ' (Gal. 2.20). This must be recaptured today, and using biblical language to illustrate sanctification can only help in this restoration process.

Wesley on Perfecting Transformation

If Wesley is known for anything, it is his faith that believers are called to be constantly transformed into the image of Christ by sanctifying grace through the ministry of the Holy Spirit. He often called this Christian perfection. Many found the doctrine of Christian perfection or perfecting grace controversial or offensive. Wesley was pressured by friend and foe alike to relinquish this tenet. He refused. He remained adamant. Why? He simply felt Christian perfection is a foundational biblical doctrine that could not be cast off without doing grievous violence to the teaching of the Scriptures. Wesley found it in the teaching of Jesus and in the Pauline, Petrine, and Johannine traditions.[21] As Tom Oden puts it, Wesley was thoroughly convinced of the following:

---

[20] Dale Coulter, 'A Wesleyan Understanding of Grace and Works', accessed online May 15, 2015, *The Seedbed Blog*, http://seedbed.com/feed/wesleyan-understanding-grace-works/.

[21] Contemporary Pentecostal biblical scholarship tends to confirm Wesley's critical insight. E.g., Adewuya, *Holiness in the Letters of Paul*, asserts that holiness is a central and essential theme in Pauline theology. Accordingly, holiness is intended to be characteristic of all believers as the Holy Spirit enables Christlike living. Therefore, holiness is not an option; rather, it is an imperative for all God's people (see p. 162).

The Spirit is determined to renew the self totally, rejecting all halfway measures. Those who are receiving regenerating grace by the Spirit are being freed not only from all outward sin at the time of new birth but also from inward sin so as to grow toward the fullness of Christ.[22]

In 'The Character of a Methodist' (Phil. 3.12; 1739) Wesley delineated the ideal of Christian perfection in action. Clearly, Christian character is not particularly recognizable by mere habits of dress and diet, adherence to political and intellectual opinions, or particular doctrinal interpretations. Character is manifested in behavior. Wholehearted love of God, unceasing prayer, serving one's neighbor in need, avoiding the allurements of the world – these are marks of Christian perfection. Christian grace and joy even in sorrowful times, lack of fear, thankfulness in all situations, lack of anxiety or despair over future security – these are marks of Christian perfection. Happiness and hopefulness in whatever state, contentment, commitment to God's will, avoiding the works of the flesh and cultivating the fruit of the Spirit, and single-minded desire for God – these are marks of Christian perfection. Continual consecration to God, commitment to practical service of others for the glory of God, in rejoicing not in fear but in gratitude – these are marks of Christian perfection. A liberated heart, delight in God's commandments, love of neighbor for God's sake, and even love of enemy, across all class or social or racial or gender lines, both in practical provision and in prayer and in taking all opportunity for doing good – these are marks of Christian perfection. A refusal to love this world order or to capitulate to its culture while valuing each person nevertheless, resisting despair and embracing only the desire of God, cleansed by God's love from every unkind temper or malignant affection – these are marks of Christian perfection. The whole life reclaimed by love, the volition totally and singly focused on God, driving out all hatred and pride and such and bringing in kindness, longsuffering, and humility with singular attention to God – these are marks of Christian perfection. In such, the kingdom/reign

---

[22] Thomas C. Oden, *Wesley's Scriptural Christianity: A Plain Exposition of His Teaching on Christian Doctrine* (Grand Rapids, MI: Zondervan Publishing, 1994), p. 320.

of God is begun. And with all of the above, there is no ground for self-congratulation – these are marks of Christian perfection.

From where did Wesley's ideal of Christian perfection come? Wesley always insisted that he preached 'plain, old Christianity' and that his idealistic description was simply what it means to be renewed in the image of God in heart and in life through Christ by the power of the Holy Spirit. This pattern of Christian perfection may be more technically described as a life shaped by unfeigned responsiveness to God. It is derived primarily from Scripture and secondarily from the Ante-Nicene Fathers. God's Word commands us to be perfect (Mt. 5.48; Heb. 6.1). Such a command apart from any possibility of compliance would be a cruel joke from a heartless tyrant. Such is not our God. God's command contains inherent promise of enabling grace. Wesley particularly admired the character of a perfect Christian drawn by Clement of Alexandria.[23] However, true to form, he desired to improve upon it by expressing it 'in a more scriptural manner'.[24]

Wesley and his preachers were sure that the Scriptures teach that God's grace extends to complete redemption, not a partial one that leaves believers still under the dominion of sin. In fact, it is a central and integral part of biblical teaching. God promised to 'redeem Israel from *all* their sins' (Ps. 130.8) and to cleanse them from impurities and idolatry (Ezek. 36.25). The Pauline portrait of the Bride of Christ is one of spotlessness and blamelessness (Eph. 5.27). Christ was manifested to destroy all the works of the devil (1 Jn 3.8). Jesus prayed that his disciples would be one and be perfect in love (Jn 17.22), and John affirmed that we are made perfect in love (1 Jn 4.17). The call and command to be perfect is given to living men and women (Mt. 5.48). Accordingly, they are continually encouraging one another to 'go on to perfection' (Heb. 6.1).

So then, Wesley does not lift up Christian perfection or entire sanctification as a goal attainable by at best a few 'super saints' that somehow surpass everyone else; rather, he describes it as the scriptural norm or standard for all Christians. In short, every child of

---

[23] 'Clement of Alexandria: Theologian of the Intelligentsia', *Christianity Today*, *accessed* March 23, 2016 from http://www.christianitytoday.com/history/peo ple/evangelistsandapologists/clement-of-alexandria.html.

[24] John Wesley, in a letter to *Lloyd's Evening Post*, March 5, 1767, in *Letters of John Wesley*, V, p. 43. See also Oden, *Wesley's Scriptural Christianity*, p. 319.

God is commanded to pursue and to walk continually toward holiness before God. Wesley here avoids the extremes of the Catholic *hierarchical and purgatorial* views of sainthood as well as the Protestant *positional and postmortem* views even as he affirms the essentials of the *biblical and patristic* views. Real, actual holiness of heart and life is available and attainable for all Christians through their humble faith in God's gracious provision.

Applications

There are similarities between the times in which we live today and those of Wesley. Now, as then, the influence of faith seems weaker than it has been previously, and the influence of evil seems to be growing in force. The need for a faith experience that transforms lives and life situations becomes much more obvious as good declines, evil spreads, and oppressive forces mount against humanity, always attacking the poor first. Like in Wesley's day, the holiness sanctification message and its experience offers potential for deliverance from such forces on all levels, individually, nationally, culturally, and with transformation for the Church. Ultimately, the time surrounding Wesley's ministry was called the Great Awakening and surely our age is overdue for such transformational intervention again.

Transformation is a label that speaks of hope. Salvation speaks of more than mercy; life can really change. Grace offers more than a seat on the transport to heaven one day; it offers a transforming journey from one level of glory to another, and another … as we walk with Christ in the Spirit here and now. God's plan holds more than forgiveness of our sins; it also holds an empowering grace to escape the dominion of sin in our lives. With this understanding of hope in the transforming power of sanctification let us determine to eschew legalism and all works righteousness as we proclaim God's intention to empower us to be holy in life.[25]

Believers today must be reminded that we have been called Christians because we have been called to be Christ-like. Many have

---

[25] As Adewuya says, *Holiness in the Letters of Paul,* there is a stark contrast between dynamic spiritual growth and transformation and 'a frantic attempt at works-righteousness' (p. 163).

forgotten that the goal of our salvation is to grow in the image of Christ. Christian leaders can take up this challenge again and encourage believers to rise up and receive grace to reach toward this prize.

It is always helpful before one runs a race to see how the course is laid out. In the same way, Christian leaders can help believers by describing the goal of the journey they are on and the critical points along the way. Our history points to crisis moments of spiritual experience with much gradual growth included in between. Whether a minister wants to see these as static points or more fluid, it will be helpful for the pilgrims on the path to understand what they can anticipate and even seek for as they journey. The *ordo salutis* must be proclaimed, described, and included often in ministry so that it becomes the subconscious expectation of all who join the journey.

One purpose of this volume is to activate conversations. Much could be discussed about looking at crisis experiences post salvation (i.e., sanctification and the baptism of the Holy Spirit) in a more fluid way. Could sanctification include an initial crisis experience with gradual growth following and which leads into a later crisis of entire sanctification? Is that initial sanctification moment at regeneration, or is there an element of surrender of self and embracing of Lordship that should be involved additionally? Could this initial step into the sanctification journey with surrender and Lordship be incorporated into water baptism, which seems natural with the text of Rom. 6.1-7? How can ministry leaders encourage and facilitate the gradual growth process in a much more effective and intentional way? What is the role of the Holy Spirit in sanctification, since he is named as an agent of sanctification in 2 Thess. 2.13 and Rom. 15.16? Many feel his work in this blessing could be emphasized more and with great benefit. Surely a description of his involvement in each step of the journey would be beneficial. From the personal journey of this writer (RH), it was Spirit baptism that was my first experience of entire sanctification. How can we allow for such fluid encounters along the *ordo salutis*? (See Chapter 6.)

Consider the Outcome

Think for a moment, what is result of viewing salvation from Wesley's perspective of the long journey as opposed to the perspective that initial conversion itself (mental assent) is the goal of the gospel. Wesley was concerned with the long journey and the formation of the image of Christ in a believer. Before starting this comparison, it must be stated that Wesley always intended that a believer would believe on Jesus Christ for the assurance of eternal life. That was what his Aldersgate experience was all about. Yet he did not give this his primary focus, since for him the long view was so much more biblical and motivational to believers.

What kind of Christians have been formed through protestant Christian ministry consistently committed to this 'short goal' of salvation by believing on Jesus? Data reveals there has been fifty years of stagnation and most recently decline in Christian faith in the western world and specifically in the former Christian nation, the United States. Certainly, these negative descriptors cannot be used to totally blame 'salvation by decision'. Yet this approach to evangelism has been the nearly uniform philosophy of reaching the lost all through these years. Nearly all statistical indicators point to the decreasing place of protestant Christianity in our culture over the last fifty years. This seems to indicate that people have been successfully called to salvation, but they have not been successfully motivated onward into a life pursuing the holiness of Christ, his perfect love, and a profound walk in the Spirit. While they have been 'saved to attend', or 'saved to sit', many have dropped out, failing to grasp the significance of this life they had been sold. And more recently data shows that the younger generation has dropped out much more radically.[26]

When we compare Wesley's approach, the words of Whitfield seem to underscore this difference. Whitfield used the term 'rope of sand' when he looked at his efforts over the years in comparison to Wesley's.[27] Could those words possibly be applied to the last fifty years of Christian ministry in the West? We greatly appreciate Bill

---

[26] See references to the research of the Barna Group, as well as references to Tyler Braun, Keith Drury, and Brett McCracken given in the Introduction.

[27] Collins, *John Wesley: A Theological Journey*, p. 123.

Hybel's humility and transparent frankness (Pastor of Willow Creek Church near Chicago, one of the largest churches in America) as he shared the findings of a study he himself commissioned to evaluate just this issue at his leading and model church here in America. They found that they had gathered new believers into the Church but that they had not had success in motivating them further into the levels of discipleship, maturity, Christian development, and Christian ministry that they intended.[28]

It may seem unfair to compare a mighty movement of God (The Great Awakening) with a prolonged period of stagnation in the West today. That must be considered. Yet, it is our presupposition that Wesley's approach for initial motivation of new believers made a radical difference. It is fair to compare George Whitfield's results with Wesley's in the same day and with the same national context. The aim of this book is to pose these questions that flow out of Wesley's ministry and his great success in building the kingdom of God. His philosophy of motivation plays a significant role.

Voices for Transformation

> Every generation has produced two kinds of Christians – the ordinary garden variety who muddle along with about as much failure as victory, but also those who have found the deeper life, the sanctified life. They have discovered a deeper experience of Christlikeness. With it comes fulfillment, joys, and satisfaction that some Christians only dream of. The hunger of your soul tells you what group you want to be a part of.[29]

'Sanctify them', literally means 'De-earth them!' That is, separate them from the earthy and the sinful transforming them to the heavenly and the holy. The Bible often compares this process to the purification of precious metals (Mal. 3.1-5). First the silver is taken from the earth and second placed in the crucible to be refined. So

---

[28] Russ Rainy, 'Summary of the Willow Creek Study', The Christian Coaching Center, http://www.christiancoachingcenter.org/index.php/russ-rainey/coa chingchurch2/, accessed Jan 2, 2016.
[29] Greathouse, *Love Made Perfect*, p. 99.

our sanctification is twofold. 'It is one thing to be taken out of the world, but quite another to have the world taken out of us'.[30]

Christ who began to live in us at conversion now reigns in us! No doubt most believers can identify with the difference between inviting Christ into our lives and the total surrender of allowing him to reign therein. In this sense, entire sanctification is the actualization of our conversion. To be truly sanctified is not to be a super Christian; it is to be a true Christian.[31] Entire sanctification purifies the heart, perfects it in the love of God and neighbor, and accelerates the believer's growth in Christlikeness.[32] We are sanctified in our consecration, separation from sin, and self-abandonment.[33]

For Wesley, belief was ultimately expressed in obedience. The test of 'knowing Christ' is whether or not we obey him ... We quickly learn that it is one thing to profess faith, but it is something else to express it.[34] Today's love, however, includes little or no accountability and makes no demands for change. Of course, such love makes a call to repentance and confession of sin antiquated and narrow minded. People say, 'If you really loved us you would not judge us'. Wesley would respond, 'It is precisely because I do love you that I call you to repent of your sins and align yourself with the will and way of God'. This is a love that confronts sin and calls for change. God's love accepts us as we are, but it does not leave us where we are.[35]

In his sermon 'The Scripture Way of Salvation', Wesley describes entire sanctification as 'love excluding sin, love filling the heart, taking up the whole capacity of the soul. How clearly does this express being perfected in love! ... For as long as love takes up the whole heart, what room is there for sin therein?'[36]

Wesley's sermon, 'A Plain Account of Christian Perfection' (1763) also supplies several significant insights. Throughout his long ministry Wesley consistently emphasized the power of the

---

[30] Greathouse, *Love Made Perfect*, pp. 116-18.

[31] Greathouse, *Love Made Perfect*, p. 59.

[32] Greathouse, *Love Made Perfect*, p. 96.

[33] Greathouse, *Love Made Perfect*, p. 92.

[34] Harper, *The Way to Heaven*, p. 50.

[35] Harper, *The Way to Heaven*, p. 99.

[36] Wesley, 'The Scripture Way of Salvation', as quoted in Harper, *The Way to Heaven*, p. 46.

Holy Spirit to completely (not partially) transform believers' lives. Wesley considered the doctrine of sanctification the 'grand depositum' of his movement, correcting the incompleteness of Luther and Calvin which in focusing on what Christ has done for us had failed to give adequate emphasis to the Holy Spirit's work in us – that is, enabling us to live a holy life.[37]

Of course, the voice of Scripture calls believers to transformation with eternal authority:

> Be perfect, therefore, as your heavenly Father is perfect (Mt. 5.48 (NRSV)

> Wherefore gird up the loins of your mind, be sober, and hope to the end for the grace that is to be brought unto you at the revelation of Jesus Christ; [14] As obedient children, not fashioning yourselves according to the former lusts in your ignorance: [15] But as he which hath called you is holy, so be ye holy in all manner of conversation; [16] Because it is written, Be ye holy; for I am holy (1 Pet. 1.13-16).

> Seeing ye have purified your souls in obeying the truth through the Spirit unto unfeigned love of the brethren, *see that ye* love one another with a pure heart fervently (1 Pet. 1.22).

> For the grace of God has appeared, bringing salvation to all, [12] training us to renounce impiety and worldly passions, and in the present age to live lives that are self-controlled, upright, and godly, [13] while we wait for the blessed hope and the manifestation of the glory of our great God and Savior, Jesus Christ. [14] He it is who gave himself for us that he might redeem us from all iniquity and purify for himself a people of his own who are zealous for good deeds (Tit. 2.11-14 (NRSV).

> Now the end of the commandment is charity out of a pure heart, and of a good conscience, and of faith unfeigned: [6] From which some having swerved have turned aside unto vain jangling; [7] Desiring to be teachers of the law; understanding neither what they say, nor whereof they affirm (1 Tim. 1.5-7).

---

[37] John Wesley, 'A Plain Account of Christian Perfection, as Believed and Taught by the Reverend Mr. John Wesley, from the Year 1725, to the Year 1777', in *Works of the Rev. John Wesley*, XI, pp. 366-445.

I appeal to you therefore, brothers and sisters, by the mercies of God, to present your bodies as a living sacrifice, holy and acceptable to God, which is your spiritual worship. [2] Do not be conformed to this world, but be transformed by the renewing of your minds, so that you may discern what is the will of God – what is good and acceptable and perfect (Rom. 12.1-2 (NRSV).

Interestingly, the word for 'conformed' in Rom. 12.2 is *syschematizo* (συσχηματίζω) and signifies to be made or shaped into a certain pattern. Think 'schema' or 'system'. However, 'transformed' is *metamorphoo* (μεταμορφόω) and signifies a change of nature or essence, or an inward change that is manifested outwardly as well. The word 'metamorphosis' has come into English from this Greek origin. A sanctification theology of transformation suggests a number of implications. First, there is a negative aspect in Christian commitment to avoid being pressed into conformity with the world system which exists in rebellion against God's righteous kingdom.

Second, there is the positive aspect of actual ontological change from a sinful, fallen condition expressed through immoral or unethical conduct into the image of God as exemplified in Christ and practically expressed in holy living through moral and ethical behavior toward God and toward other human beings.

Third, since neither of the two above can be accomplished by human ability, the grace of God in Christ and the power of the Holy Spirit effect transformation/sanctification as one believes the promise of full salvation and yields him/herself to God.

Finally, sanctifying transformation has a beginning (initiation), development (maturation), and objective or goal (consummation). Taken together, this process signifies Christian perfection as a biblically based and theologically informed way of life in this world in preparation for the world to come.

John Wesley's Prayer

Lord, You who did not please Yourself, even though You created all things for Your pleasure; let some portion of Your Spirit descend on me so I may deny myself and follow You. Strengthen my soul that I may exercise temperance in all things, that I may never use any part of Your creation except for a purpose You command me to pursue, and in the

measure and manner which most promotes that
heaven-sent goal.

Do not allow me to gratify the desires which do not have
You as their ultimate object.

Let me always abstain from pleasures which do not prepare
me for taking pleasure in You, knowing that all such war
against the soul and tend to alienate from You.

Do save me from indulging in the desire of the flesh, the
desire of the eye, or the pride of life.

Set a watch, O Lord, over my senses and appetites, my passions and understanding, that I may resolutely deny them
every gratification which has no tendency to Your glory.

Do train me in the good way, so that when I am old I may
not depart from it, that I may be, at length, a truly humble
heart, crucified to the world and the world crucified to me.
Amen.[38]

---

[38] Wesley, *Wesley's Daily Prayers*, p. 88.

4

FORMATION

Christianity is a social religion and to turn it into a solitary one is to destroy it.[1] – John Wesley

I am more and more convinced that the devil himself desires nothing more than this, that the people of any place should be half awakened and then left to themselves to fall asleep again. Therefore, I determine, by the grace of God, not to strike one stroke in any place where I cannot follow the blow.[2] – John Wesley

Nurture in Groups

Second only to Wesley's teaching on entire sanctification, or Christian perfection, we recognize his ministry strategy of gathering new converts (and even the unconverted) into small groups for nurture toward spiritual growth. Actually, we understand there were three expressions of this idea of gathering believers together. First was the 'society', next the 'class', and then the 'band'. The society was like a church meeting, even though Wesley was not aiming to start his own church. He did feel it was necessary to bring his followers together to hear the Word of God as the faith of the Methodists would proclaim it. It is a point of interest that most of the Meth-

---

[1] Collins, *John Wesley: A Theological Journey*, p. 83.

[2] John Wesley, *The Works of John Wesley* (ed. R.E. Davies; Nashville: Abingdon Press, Bicentennial edn, 1989), IX, pp. 222-23. As quoted in Collins, *John Wesley*, p. 328.

odists that regularly attended society meetings also faithfully attended the Church of England in their community, especially to receive sacraments. Though Wesley was accused of both starting a
movement outside the Anglican church and taking people from the
Church, it is quite possible his followers helped to augment attendance at declining Anglican services.

The 'Holy Club' at Oxford in Wesley's early years was his first
attempt at creating a nurturing group. That youthful group had
rules to be followed by all members and they saw themselves as
believers committed to more rigorous spiritual discipline based on
the example of the primitive church as they understood it. They
prayed together, fasted twice a week, read and studied the Bible together (often in the Greek New Testament) attended sacraments
regularly, collected money for the poor, as well as visiting the prison,
teaching orphans, and helping the poor.[3] Actually, Wesley and the
'Holy Club' were the first ones to be called Methodists due to these
'methods' that the group maintained in their efforts to grow in spiritual maturity and fruit. Most of these elements were also found
subsequently in the Methodist societies and class groups that filled
England from 1738 and beyond. The specific purposes for societies
and classes were Christian instruction and to watch over one another in love, to help each other work out their own salvation.[4]

The next level of group meeting was the 'class meeting'. It is this
meeting that seemed to be the heart of the nurture Methodism is
so well known for. The classes were smaller in size and would most
often meet in homes. It was through the class structure that pastoral
care was given, including more personal aid in spiritual development. The class meetings were required of everyone that wanted to
join a society and they typically included prayer, Bible study, mutual
confession, and support. It has been said that in these meetings
many disenfranchised people of England 'found their voice'. They
learned that God was listening to them, and so they learned to pray,
even extemporaneous prayers from the heart, beyond the Anglican
prayer book. They learned that God was speaking to them, even in
their lowly state of life, and so they learned to read and study the
Bible. They learned that their brothers and sisters in Christ loved

---

[3] Runyon, *The New Creation*, p. 117.
[4] Collins, *John Wesley: A Theological Journey*, p. 121.

them and so they shared their successes and struggles with a new-found family. Obviously, powerful social forces were at play as these new converts from the lowest depths of society 'found their voice' as well as their footing, and began to climb out of poverty's oppression lifted by this marvelous saving, sanctifying, and delivering grace.[5]

The final expression of the small group structure created by Wesley was the 'band'. This was a voluntary small group composed of same sex and same marital status individuals for the purpose of sharing more intimately and encouraging one another more specifically in the walk of holy living. Each member was encouraged to 'speak as freely, plainly, and concisely as he could, the real state of his heart, with his several temptations and deliverances since the last time of the meeting'.[6] Often the sharing focused on simple questions, such as, 'What sin have you committed since the last meeting? Are you hiding anything that you do not want to be known? Does any sin have control of you?'[7]

Obviously, these meetings were much more personal and rigorous, with leaders and group members committed to help struggling members walk through temptations and gain freedom over specific sins. The band meetings did not continue on as long as the society and class meetings did in the history of early Methodism. No doubt there were psychological barriers that in time became too great for members to hurdle. In such an open format, the benefits could be great and the potential for difficulties great as well. Nevertheless, the 'band meeting' concept was a part of the vibrant ministry carried forward in the Methodist movement from the 1740's.

A Social Faith

Certainly, Wesley's words demonstrate his deep conviction about the relational key to faith, 'Christianity is a social religion and to turn it into a solitary one is to destroy it'.[8] That is pretty strong. And listen to his words of warning later in life. 'Without this religious

---

[5] Runyon, *The New Creation*, pp. 119-21.
[6] Runyon, *The New Creation*, p. 122.
[7] Collins, *John Wesley: A Theological Journey*, p. 122.
[8] Collins, *John Wesley: A Theological Journey*, p. 83.

connection and intercourse, the most ardent attempts, by mere preaching, have proved no lasting use'.[9] In Wesley's sermon, 'The Work of God in North America', he spoke about converts that had no such relational connections.

> They had no shadow of discipline; nothing of the kind. They were formed into no societies. They had no Christian connection with each other, nor were ever taught to watch over each other's souls. So if they fell into lukewarmness, or even into sin, he had none to lift him up. [10]

Clearly for Wesley the private weekly meeting for prayer, examination, and exhortation was the greatest means to keep and confirm every blessing received by the preached word.

Wesley's conviction is supported by the biblical description of the Church, as well as the very nature of the Holy Trinity. Scripture reveals God as self-communicating love. It is love that is the ultimate expression of God, the social Trinity. Self-communication is the very nature of God; and, therefore, this social relating is an essential characteristic of the Church. 'Spirituality as restoration of *Imago Dei* implies a life that reflects or mirrors in social relationships the actual relational life of God in Trinity'.[11] The church is identified in the New Testament as the Body of Christ. Therefore, like Christ in the Trinity, the members are to be intricately connected with functions intertwined and purposes all complementing the overarching Body life, synergistically contributing together as one, yet diverse.

Wesley understood this concept of the Church was essential and powerful. Consider Eph. 4.16 (with notations in brackets):

> From whom [Christ] the whole body [not simply individuals] fitly joined together and compacted by that which every joint

---

[9] Wesley, *The Works of John Wesley* (ed. T. Jackson), XI, p. 433. As cited in Harper, *The Way to Heaven*, p. 136.

[10] Wesley, *The Works of John Wesley* (ed. T. Jackson), VII, p. 411. As cited in Harper, *The Way to Heaven*, p. 134.

[11] Johns, 'The Practice of Holiness', p. 109. Johns mentions additional works supporting this social concept: Catherine Mowry LaCugna, *God for Us: The Trinity and Christian Life* (San Francisco: Harper, 1991), p. 271; Miroslav Volf, *After Our Likeness: The Church as the Image of the Trinity* (Grand Rapids, Eerdmans, 1998), p. 207; and Jürgen Moltmann, *The Trinity and the Kingdom of God* (Minneapolis: Fortress Press, 1993), p. 161.

supplies [requires connecting/sharing/relating], according to the effectual working [*energia* is only used in the NT for super human power][12] in the measure of every part, makes increase of the body [growth spiritually and growth numerically] unto the edifying of itself [caring for and building up one another] in love.

Notice the word *energia* (ἐνέργεια), translated 'effectual working'. Paul understood that the super natural power of God was released from Christ when the components of this seemingly complicated scriptural passage come together. When the parts are fitly joined together, this cannot happen without intentional connecting. When the parts are compacted by the supply every part contributes, sharing of many kinds among all the members activate this. All these body members build one another up and release divine power as this inter-relating takes place. And naturally this causes great personal spiritual growth, which will often bring some level of numerical growth, as a natural bi-product. Wesley saw this connecting/relating as the critical element that could not be ignored in the development (sanctification) of each new believer. He shows this strong commitment when he said, 'I determine, by the grace of God, not to strike one stroke in any place where I cannot follow the blow'.[13]

Means of Grace

Continued spiritual growth in all of the dimensions of life was the grand goal toward which all of Wesley's energies moved. Wesley said,

> Nothing can be more plain, than that the life of God in the soul does not continue, much less increase, unless we use all opportunities of communion with God, and pouring out our hearts before him. If, therefore, we are negligent of this ... life will surely decay.[14]

[12] Joseph Thayer, *Thayer's Greek-English Lexicon of the New Testament* (New York: Hendrickson, 1996).
[13] Wesley, *The Works of John Wesley* (ed. Davies), IX, pp. 222-23. As quoted in Collins, *John Wesley*, p. 328.
[14] Chilcote, *Recapturing the Wesleys' Vision*, p. 71.

William Greathouse illustrates this decay due to lack of nurture with a simple illustration of a gazelle.

'In my dream,' a man told his pastor, 'I approach a cage filled with wild animals. In the front of the cage are voracious lions, tigers, and bears. In the back of the cage is a gentle, graceful, gazelle. I keep trying to feed the gazelle, but the fierce animals in the front keep devouring all of the food. In the end the starving gazelle grows weak and dies.' The pastoral counselor told him, 'The gazelle is your true self, your best self – the part of you that is created in the image of God. The lions, tigers, and bears are perhaps greed, anger, passion, lust, and so on, that are starving that which is best in your life.'

The genius of John Wesley was to devise a ministry structure that would encourage believers of all types to nurture the life of Christ that had been born within at regeneration. One of the most critical ingredients in Wesley's strategy for nurturing converts in his groups was instructing them and motivating them in participating in the 'means of grace'. For Wesley, the means of grace included 'works of piety' and 'works of mercy'. Works of piety were directed toward God just as the Great Commandment says, Thou shalt love the Lord your God with all your heart, and with all your soul, and with all your mind (Mt. 22.37). The works of piety included scripture reading and study, prayer, sacraments, fasting, and Christian conversation or conference, where believers shared one to another about their struggles and successes in defeating and dealing with sin in their lives.[15]

While works of piety were directed toward God, works of mercy were directed toward others as in the second great commandment that Jesus mentioned: 'Thou shalt love your neighbor as thyself. On these two commandments hang all the Law and the Prophets' (Mt. 22.39-40). Works of mercy included a wide spectrum of acts to love and serve others, with specific focus on the poor, the sick, those in prisons, the aged, or the young. Works of mercy will receive attention in the next chapter, though it must be underscored here that the works of mercy were seen as genuine avenues to grace for believers whereby they might grow in sanctification.

---

[15] Chilcote, *Recapturing the Wesleys' Vision*, p. 71.

Wesley believed that the 'means of grace' were effective to activate grace in the life of the believer. With his sights set on the *telos* of salvation, Christian perfection in holy love, rather than on the conversion experience, Wesley felt new believers and all believers needed to be participating actively in these channels of grace to continue their journey of sanctification toward holy love and full formation in the image of God. Only grace could achieve such an end, and the means of grace brought direct and regular access to such grace. Wesley knew that continued access to grace would build up and fortify God's work in any life, while at the same time diminishing the strength of carnality.

The long-term result of contact with grace through the means of grace is growth in the divine nature (2 Pet. 1.2-4). Remember, while the means of grace are discussed, that Wesley built every aspect of his theology on love,[16] loving God and loving others. With this foundation, the means of grace become avenues to know God more and more rather than legalistic formulas. Spending time in God's Word means hearing his voice in Scripture. Prayer means talking to God and listening in God's presence. The sacraments became moments of divine encounter and divine infusion. Fasting was setting aside nourishment to focus most intensely on seeking God, just as Christ had modeled.[17] Christian conference was a way to relate with believers emulating Christ relating in the Trinity. Works of mercy were the way to walk in the footsteps of Christ and to go to where Christ was, among the broken and hurting. Clearly relating motivated by love is fundamental to Wesley's concept of the 'means of grace'.

Catechism Model and Motivation

In many ways, Wesley's group ministry for the formation of believers (societies, classes, and bands) seems to draw much from the model of the baptismal instruction that the early church used to

---

[16] Wynkoop, *Theology of Love*, p 76.

[17] For a detailed discussion of Wesley's views on fasting, see Lee Roy Martin, *Fasting: A Centre for Pentecostal Theology Short Introduction* (Cleveland, TN: CPT Press, 2014), pp. 110-14.

prepare new converts for baptism, but more fundamentally, for living out this new way of life and participation in the family of God (catechism). Of course, those were primary goals for Wesley's group ministry even as he built them into the framework of growth and development toward 'entire sanctification'. We know from the 'Wesleyan Quadrilateral' that tradition was a significant factor in his decision-making process (Scripture, tradition, reason, and experience).[18] We also know that Wesley was a keen student of the Early Church Fathers who were deeply committed to this early training model, who developed it, and who laid this foundation for church history (Origen, Clement, Tertullian, Augustine, to name only a few). And a brief scan of church history would reveal that Wesley's group ministry structure was one of the most successful adaptations of the catechism model since the days of the Early Fathers. With these points of connection in mind we will consider a few similarities between the catechism model and Wesley's group ministry structure.

First there is agreement that new believers need further intensive instruction and guidance to successfully enter the life of faith and the life of the Church. After all, this theme is given in the second half of Christ's Great Commission to his church: 'teaching them to obey everything that I have commanded you' (Mt. 28.19–20 NIV). From the early church the *Didascalia Apostolorum* says, 'When the heathen desire and promise to repent, saying "We believe," we receive them into the congregation so that they may hear the word, but do not receive them into communion until they receive the seal and are fully initiated' (2.39).[19] We see here that the early church used baptism as a motivating factor, in that new believers must receive catechism as preparation for their baptism, which was for them the sacrament and ceremony for entrance into the Body of Christ. The church also used Communion as a motivating factor, in

---

[18] See Don Thorsen, *The Wesleyan Quadrilateral: Scripture, Tradition, Reason, and Experience as a Model of Evangelical Theology* (Lexington, KY: Emeth Press, 2005 edition [originally 1990]).

[19] Clinton E. Arnold, 'Early Church Catechesis and New Christians' Classes in Contemporary Evangelicalism', *Journal of the Evangelical Theological Society* 47.1 (March 2004), pp. 39-54 (p. 42). Arnold was professor of New Testament at Talbot School of Theology, La Mirada, CA. This paper is a revised form of the Presidential Address given at the annual meeting of the Far West Region of the Evangelical Theological Society on May 2, 2003.

that new believers would only be ready to receive communion with the community of faith after the catechism.

Wesley was more subtle than the Early Fathers; still, he understood the power of motivation to help keep people moving along the path of spiritual development. Consider three subtle motivations for Wesley. The first seems most intriguing for modern faith. As Wesley proclaimed the Word in large open air meetings, often his call to the people was different. Very often he called them to join a small group, a class that was meeting or forming in the area. So even before bringing them through the threshold of faith in Christ, Wesley was drawing them into a group for formation that would lead them to Christ but that would also lead them onward toward greater sanctifying experience. Subtly in his call, Wesley was guiding them to a forming group using their desire for assurance of faith in Christ as motivation. The record of the Methodist periodical, *The Arminian*, shows that unbelievers would participate in those groups for an average of more than two years before coming to full assurance of faith.[20] This is quite different from our model today where we load salvation by faith in Christ on the front end of everything we do and it often degenerates into mental assent, passivity, and spiritual recidivism.

Second, Wesley was subtly motivating his people onward by placing the communion service, the preaching of the Word, and gathering with the larger body of the faithful in a second step, the society meeting. All of those attending a class meeting were given a card which became their pass for entrance into the society meeting. If a Methodist was not willing to participate in the personal growth process of a class meeting then they would not be allowed to participate in the society meeting. In a humorous anecdotal note, Wesley himself was denied access to a society meeting on one occasion because he did not have a 'class card' to show that day.

Third, Wesley constantly held out the invitation to Christian perfection through entire sanctification. We realize these are not terms our culture is comfortable with today and so we will need to find other terms that capture the essence of Scripture's strong call to become like Christ and to be filled with holy love in very genuine ways. Nevertheless, this call was similar to the catechism model of

---

[20] Runyon, *The New Creation*, p. 115.

the Early Church Fathers who aimed to motivate new converts through intense spiritual development in the first three years or so of their faith walk. Quite obviously, these elements of motivation were successful for both the early church and for Wesley as Christian history records their impact. For both the Early Fathers and Wesley, the motivation for a lengthy process was rooted in a desire to foster solid spiritual formation and to protect these new believers against sin, heresy, and apostasy.[21] We can learn from such models.

Common Keys

Clinton Arnold found in his study of the early church catechumenate that there were four key elements found in most expressions, even in diverse geographic areas. Those were (1) teaching new converts the Word of God in a thorough systematic manner, (2) teaching the central doctrines of the Church, (3) guiding candidates in spiritual and moral formation, and (4) laying hands on them for deliverance from all evil of the world as they enter the communion of the Church. These elements were built into a lengthy, often three-year curriculum for new converts before they were baptized and inducted into the community of faith. In that time frame most of the major themes of the Bible could be taught as well as many of the fundamental doctrines of Christianity. Each new convert was assigned a spiritual mentor to walk with them week-by-week through the catechesis period where real and profound spiritual and moral development issues could be addressed. As a conclusion to this development, the catechesis process included a deliverance component intended to assure that new candidates were aided to be free from all influences of their dark past and could step into the Body of Christ purged and free.[22]

Wesley was obviously just as convinced as the Early Fathers of the need for intense training, relating, and development for the new converts and interested people attracted to the gospel. His structure for group ministry and personal growth in grace included these same components that were central to the catechesis process. Naturally Wesley's program was greatly modified from the process

---

21 Arnold, 'Early Church Catechesis and New Christians' Classes', p. 44.
22 Arnold, 'Early Church Catechesis and New Christians' Classes', pp. 46-52.

found in the catechism, yet the four critical elements that Arnold describes are seen with adaptations in Wesley's groups. Preaching and teaching of the Word was emphasized in the society meetings, which were held weekly. Teaching the central doctrines of the Church was not as structured or intentional in Wesley's groups, though his training requirements for the Methodist preachers was extensive in biblical doctrine, original text study, and reading the writings of church fathers.

Spiritual and moral formation was a central tenant for Wesley. This was natural since development in the graces of entire sanctification was the core motivation of his process. The class leaders and band leaders performed much the same function as the mentors of the catechesis model, walking beside the new converts and guiding them through spiritual and moral dilemmas as needed. In Wesley's process, deliverance was more of an ongoing work relying on continued exposure to the 'means of grace', such as the preached Word, reading the Word, the sacraments, prayer, fasting, and Christian conversation (sharing personally and intimately with a leader and other believers). Though Wesley's approach was different, *The Arminian* often wrote of lives being radically transformed by the power of grace as people participated in the Methodist group ministries.

Naturally there were great differences between the Wesley program and the early church catechism. Possibly the most obvious was that Wesley prescribed his group ministry system for all Methodists, both unconverted, new converts, and mature believers. Of course Wesley's commitment to lifelong growth in sanctification made it natural to expect that all believers needed to take advantage of the group development offered there. In the same line of reasoning, Wesley's groups were not for a defined period of time which culminated in graduation, or entrance into the community of faith. Wesley held deep convictions that there was no end to the possibilities for spiritual growth; and, therefore, all believers ought to be constantly participating in the growth process with others. Continued growth in all of the dimensions of life was the grand goal toward which all of Wesley's energies moved. Wesley's words can be repeated here,

Nothing can be more plain, than that the life of God in the soul does not continue, much less increase, unless we use all opportunities of communion with God, and pouring out our hearts before him. If, therefore, we are negligent of this - life will surely decay.[23]

George Whitfield was impressed with the lasting results of Wesley and he later attributed Wesley's greater success to the class meetings. He said, 'The souls awakened under Wesley's ministry, he joined in class meetings, and preserved the fruits of his labor. This I neglected, and my people are a rope of sand'.[24]

Equal to preaching was the ministry of small groups in the Methodist structure. They demonstrate the philosophy that Christianity is more caught that taught. The claim is valid for Methodists that evangelism took place as much in the intimacy of the small group as in the major preaching events. Wesley said, 'I was more convinced than ever that preaching like an apostle, without joining together those that are awaken and training them up in the ways of God, is only begetting children for the murder room'. The definitive organism of early Methodist ministry was the small group meeting. Dedicated people learned to grow in Christ, learned the depths of God's love for them, and learned the witness of loving service to one another and to others that defined Methodist evangelism.[25]

Applications

Wesley was convinced that he needed a 'method' to lead people on from their salvation/justification experience, moving constantly forward toward the goal of God's image being fully formed in believers. His results are recorded in history and now over 200 years later we continue to talk about the impact of those 'Methodists'. Today pastors need a new, relevant, and current-day applicable 'method' that they can use to lead their people on beyond justification toward the goal of Christ's image and Holy love, in the fashion of Wesley. He knew that people often follow the form of religion without the power, but he also observed that when people left the

---

[23] Chilcote, *Recapturing the Wesleys' Vision*, p. 73.
[24] Collins, *John Wesley: A Theological Journey*, p. 123.
[25] Chilcote, *Recapturing the Wesleys' Vision*, p. 100.

form of religion their power often diminished. Wesley was convinced that when the form and power of religion was held together believers experienced true 'fellowship with God, the living power of faith divine'.[26] Surely today we could agree, offering some path for believers to walk aimed at growth in sanctification would be better than no method at all.

Certainly, the kernel at the heart of Wesley's methods was a life of personal devotion, love for and hunger for Christ. Before any concern for developing structures for practicing the 'means of grace' it would be good to declare that the foundation of all progress in the sanctification journey is personal devotion to Christ (loving God). Wesley was primarily concerned with developing a faith that worked in everyday living. He was a person of intense and meaningful discipline. Everyday counted; every moment was a God moment. Consequently, he gave himself daily to the spiritual disciplines of prayer, Bible study, and devotion. Wesley said, 'The soul and body make the man, and the Spirit and discipline make the Christian'. Wesley's life and theology pulsate with the word daily. For over sixty years he faithfully engaged in devotional living. He calls us to do the same.[27]

The heart of Wesley's method was the 'means of grace'. In his mind these activities were fountains of grace and all who participated in these would receive grace infusions to lift them further toward the great goal of Christ's image. One recommendation would be for pastors to lead a season of emphasis regularly/annually on participation in the means of grace. This could be applied with great variety in churches, but the goal would be for the people to be greatly encouraged in an intensive season to get involved in several of the means of grace. As one specific example, this could look like a call to the Church to pray and fast in more concentrated ways during the season of Lent or to begin a New Year. The goal would be to greatly increase involvement in various 'works of piety' and the pastor could even plan opportunities to experience the 'works of mercy' during this special called season. Numerous variations and expansions of this concept could be attempted. Wesley was

---

[26] Chilcote, *Recapturing the Wesleys' Vision*, p. 56.

[27] Wesley, *The Works of John Wesley* (ed. T. Jackson), p. 14. As cited in in Harper, *The Way to Heaven*, p. 76.

deeply convinced that growth in grace is not accidental or automatic. One does not wonder or stumble into maturity. On God's side, he does not save us and then tell us to do the best we can. Rather, he supplies specific instruments through which he can nurture us. To be sure, he is not limited to these means, but he has chosen to use them as his primary and normal means of effecting Christian growth. Wesley felt it would be difficult to meet a vital growing Christian who did not use these means of grace in one way or another.

We know that Wesley's great achievement was gathering believers together in groups with the purpose of growing in their experience with Christ. One recommendation would be for a church to plan one significant Bible Study or Christian Education study that targets this concept. We suggest this was the precise goal of Henry Blackaby's *Experiencing God* and a concomitant benefit of Rick Warren's *Purpose Driven Life*. No doubt numerous other authors have written in this vein. We are thinking of Francis Chan's *Crazy Love*, and *Yawning at Tigers* by Drew Dyck, or classics like Richard Foster's *Celebration of Discipline*, or Dallas Willard's *The Spirit of the Disciplines*. The idea here is to begin to consistently sow the idea into the Church that we are serious about growing in the image of Christ and we are planning moments of ministry that will encourage believers along this journey.[28]

Next it could be recommended that the Church start some kind of discipleship groups within the Church (as Wesley started societies, classes, and bands within the Anglican church). We like the phrase *God Chasers* that Thomas Tenney used as a title for his book. That title certainly could have been applied to Wesley's 'Holy Club' early in his Oxford days. It captures the thrust and trajectory of Wesley's motivation to pursue far more than the justification experience. This group could be set up for similar purposes as the 'Holy Club', with structure and methods to be followed, which would help each member actively grow in their walk with God. A modification to this could take a page right out of Jesus' own ministry. We could

---

[28] Consider these sources: Henry Blackaby and Claude King, *Experiencing God* (Nashville: B&H Publishing, 2008); Rick Warren, *The Purpose Driven Life* (Grand Rapids: Zondervan, 2002); Francis Chan, *Crazy Love* (Colorado Springs: David C. Cook, 2008); Drew Dyck, *Yawning at Tigers* (Nashville: Nelson, 2014); Tommy Tenney, *God Chasers* (Shippensburg, PA: Destiny Image, 1998).

start a single group of those in the Church that volunteer as believers hungry to grow and be transformed. These believers would walk through 'Class' and 'Band' type experiences to prove the potential to avoid conformation to the world and pursue transformation to Christ. When this group experiences success, then there will likely be testimonies of the product desired so that the leaders can then call others to join the movement. Also, from that first group will come leaders for the second generation groups and so on.

Variations on the group growth theme could be wide. As an example, when we began to read about Wesley's groups we were immediately reminded of the 'Celebrate Recovery' movement.[29] John Baker's book sounds like stories from revivals of past generations. The stories of lives completely turned around from addictions sounded just like testimonies coming from great revival meetings of earlier days. Of course, now this ministry makes us think of Wesley's 'classes' and 'bands' where the unconverted join the group and in time they are converted and transformed by God's grace. Another example of diversity in application would be creating groups along homogenous lines by interest, or by careers, or by life/age range, or by skills, or by a sense of specific ministry calling (i.e. music, youth, children, evangelism, social outreach, etc.). Care must be given to maintain the central purpose of spiritual development through the 'means of grace' toward white hot 'Holy Love', the image of Christ, and entire sanctification.

The ability of groups to be effective in evangelism is proven. David Yongi Cho in Seoul Korea has used cell ministry to multiply ministry massively. The G-12 movement launched by Harold Caballeros of the El Shadai church in Central America is another massive example. More will be said about 'mobilization' in connection with the sanctifying journey in the next chapter.

Sharing testimonies was a vital aspect of Wesley's groups and has benefit that is possibly overlooked today. The practice of testimony is formative for groups. Public testimonies benefit the testifier by confirming his or her experience with God on the sanctification journey. They also benefit those that receive the testimony

---

[29] John Baker and Rick Warren, *Celebrate Recovery* (Saddleback, CA: Saddleback Resources, 2007). Numerous resources have been developed in the *Celebrate Recovery* line. Look for these online at www.saddlebackresources.com.

by holding up the hope of and means for progress in one's sanctification. At the heart of the Wesleyan/Holiness tradition is the
commitment to concrete holiness as a real possibility in this life.
Public testimony demonstrates this possibility and without such testimony the call to holiness is empty. It is fitting that we see in Wesley's groups the power and effectiveness of testimony (sharing together), encouraging one another by speaking of one's victories
through struggles toward further sanctification. The decline in the
practice of testimony can be closely linked with the decline in interest in pursuing holiness through sanctification. The practice of
testimony is formative for communities by keeping the possibility
of entire sanctification alive and fresh as group members share
from their current life experiences.[30]

Clinton Arnold writes about application of the catechesis model
for today:

> The most natural place for this to occur is in the context of re-
> lationships built either in a small group setting or in a mentoring
> relationship. Earning respect and the right to be heard is crucial
> for effectiveness in gently but firmly speaking into the life of a
> new believer. A hard question that we need to ask of ourselves
> is whether there is an intentional and structured part of the cur-
> riculum for ministering to new believers in our churches that ad-
> dresses issues of life-style and Christian behavior in a direct way.
> Is there a process that helps new believers confront and deal
> with such sin issues as sexual impurity, bitterness, rebellion,
> greed, and unforgiveness, as well as cultic involvements and ad-
> herence to false religious beliefs?[31]

---

[30] John L. Drury, 'Barth and Testimony', in Christian T. Collins Winn and
John L. Drury (eds.), *Karl Barth and the Future of Evangelical Theology* (Eugene, OR:
Wipf and Stock Pub., 2014), p. 106. Might this be comparable to the loss of the
testimony service, often straightforward and uncomfortable, in contemporary
Pentecostalism? See Tony Richie, 'Spiritual Transformation through Pentecostal
Testimony', in David S.E. Han and Jackie David Johns (eds.), *Knowing God in the
Ordinary Practices of the Christian Life* (Cleveland, TN: CPT Press, forthcoming).
Cp. R. Lamar Vest and Steve Land, *Reclaiming Your Testimony: Your Story and the
Christian Story* (Cleveland, TN: Pathway Press, 2002).

[31] Arnold, 'Early Church Catechesis and New Christians' Classes', p. 51.

Arnold also gives a challenge to the ministry leaders today as he looks at the commitment of the church fathers of the stature of Augustine to teach the catechumenate:

> Teaching new converts was a top priority for Christian scholars of that day. As we consider the lives and writings of the most well-known church leaders in the first four centuries, it is amazing how many of them devoted themselves to the task of teaching new believers [Origen, Clement, Tertullian, Augustine, etc.]. If the training of new believers was such an important ministry in the estimation of the well-known leaders and teachers of the ancient church, it is natural to ask whether it is equally a priority among the scholars and Bible teachers of our time. How many seminary professors are teaching in the functional equivalent of a catechumenate? How many evangelical pastors?[32]

To conclude this segment on formation, Roberta Bondi speaks from the practice of the ancient church about growing in the love of God:

> We all expect to love our neighbor from the day we become Christian, and we also expect to love God. Unfortunately, our expectations usually have almost nothing to do with what happens. Many of us have no sense of God at all, or if we do, it is more like a sense of duty or even fear toward God. Then, because we believe we should love God, we judge ourselves to be religious failures.

> Our ancestors made no such assumptions about Christian love. Gregory of Nyssa, for example, characterized the life of the monk in three stages. At the beginning, she or he serves God out of fear, like a slave; next, the service of God stems from the desire for a reward, like that of a hired hand. Only in the final stage does this person serve God out of friendship with God, or out of the pure love of God, as a child of God's household. The significant point here for us is that the love of God is conceived of as being difficult, something to be learned over a very long time. In fact, this is what ascetic discipline was designed to do: to train it's practitioners in the ways of God, so that, if God

---

[32] Arnold, 'Early Church Catechesis and New Christians' Classes', p. 45.

should put that love into their hearts, they might come truly to love God and God's images, other people ... This is still one of the most potentially significant lessons the ancient church has to teach us today.[33]

John Wesley's Prayer

O Savior of all who trust in You, do with what seems best in Your own eyes, only give me the mind of Christ. Let me learn from You how to be meek and humble, pouring into me the spirit of humility. Fill, I ask You most fervently, every part of my soul, and make Your Spirit the constant, ruling habit of my mind. Make all emotions rise from Your Spirit. I want no thoughts, no desires, no designs, but what come truly from You. Amen.[34]

---

[33] Bondi, *To Love as God Loves*, pp. 27-28.
[34] Wesley, *Wesley's Daily Prayers*, p. 87.

5

MOBILIZATION

Do all the good you can, by all the means you can, in all the ways you can, in all the places you can, at all the times you can, to all the people you can, as long as ever you can.[1] – Anonymous

[The person] who sins against [the neighbor] does evil to [the self]; and [the person] who does good to [the] neighbor, does good to [the self].[2]
– Saint Anthony

Holiness in Mission

The Father consecrated the Son and sent him into the world, so now the Son sanctifies/consecrates the Church and sends them into the world. 'The church exists by mission as fire exists by burning'. (Emil Brunner) When fire ceases to burn, it ceases to be. So when the Church does not burn with a passion to make Christ known to the world, it ceases to be the Church – and becomes either a sect like the Pharisees or a social club! The Church is the only institution on earth that exists primarily for non-members! It exists chiefly, Jesus reminds us, so that the

---

[1] John Anderson, 'Things John Wesley Never Said', http://www.jonathan an-dersen.com/things-john-wesley-never-said/, accessed online March 20, 2016. Anderson notes that this quote has been attributed to Wesley so often that most believe it was Wesley that said it. He mentions in this article that Richard Heit-zenrater has written, 'Many of the quotations cited to Wesley simply sound like something he might have said or written, rather than being something he actually expressed'.

[2] Bondi, *To Love as God Loves*, p. 28.

world may know that thou hast sent me and hast loved them, even as thou hast loved me (Jn 17.23).[3]

The primary question for the Wesley Methodist was not am I saved? The ultimate question was, '… for what purpose?' Wesley taught that the neighbor is the goal of our redemption just as the life and death of Christ is oriented toward the salvation of all humanity. The fundamental vision of Christian mission is being 'sent' to continue and participate in the movement of God toward humanity that began with the mission of sending Christ and the Holy Spirit. Christ's mission was characterized by healing the sick, liberating the oppressed, and caring for the poor. In all of these actions the Church incarnates shalom, God's vision of peace, justice, and well-being for all. If evangelism has to do with bringing people into the fold of God's love and care, then mission refers to the outward movement of God's people into places where lonely people dwell.[4] Wesley wrote that he believed the heart of the gospel, the substance of its many liberating graces, would not be actualized – but through mission.[5]

David Martin said in his book, *Pentecostalism: The World Their Parish*:

We have in Pentecostalism … the religious mobilization of the culturally despised, above all in the non-western world, outside any sponsorship whatever … John Wesley and his associates started it, out of materials provided by Pietism. The evangelical revival then set off further mobilizations which in the course of experimentation cross bred the religion of poor whites with the religion of poor blacks to create a potent and ambiguous mix capable of combustion on a global scale. Wesley had, after all, declared that his message was to all, not just the elect.[6]

While Robert Mapes Anderson obviously overstated his sociological argument that early Pentecostalism essentially arose as a reactionary movement against social and economic deprivation, he is at least correct to the extent that early Pentecostals definitely acted

---

[3] Greathouse, *Love Made Perfect*, p. 119.
[4] Chilcote, *Recapturing the Wesleys' Vision*, p. 101.
[5] Collins, *John Wesley: A Theological Journey*, p. 55.
[6] David Martin, *Pentecostalism: The World Their Parish*, quoted by Knight III (ed.), *From Aldersgate to Azusa Street*, p. 2.

out of concern for the marginalized masses.[7] But have Pentecostals continued this compassionate tradition of Wesley into the present with the ardor and energy he would have affirmed?

Loving Compassion

During the ministry of Wesley in England, working conditions were often unsafe and unhealthy, and women and children as well as men often worked 12-15 hour days, six days a week, just to make a subsistence wage. Living conditions were no better, and many lives were marked by poverty, alcoholism, disease, and illiteracy. John Wesley and his Methodists would engage in a wide range of ministries to these workers, including literacy classes, health care, and providing such basic necessities as food, clothing, and shelter.[8]

To develop holiness, Wesley encouraged spiritual disciplines in devotional life, sacramental piety, AND ministering to the poor. These holistic activities also marked the Oxford holy club, or Methodists, as they were called even that early, visiting prisons, and teaching orphans.[9] Is it possible that this concept has been greatly lost to current day Christian practice? Wesley believed that participating in efforts to help needy people was an avenue to develop oneself in holiness. Today we see clearly that loving God is the way to holiness, but Wesley also saw that loving others that are made in the image of God was a way to access greater sanctifying grace, becoming more like Christ.

Works of Mercy

Wynkoop well says,

> Holiness, to Wesley, could not ignore, or become insensitive to, or withdraw from one's fellows. Here again the nature of love as the meaning of holiness prevailed over any ascetic or less worthy

---

[7] Robert Mapes Anderson, *Vision of the Disinherited: The Making of American Pentecostalism* (Oxford: Oxford University Press, 1979).

[8] Henry H. Knight III, 'The Eighteenth Century: The Birth of Methodism', in Knight III (ed.), *From Aldersgate to Azusa Street*, p. 13.

[9] Henry H. Knight III, 'John Wesley and the Quest for Holiness', in Knight III (ed.), *From Aldersgate to Azusa Street*, p. 18.

concept. The evidence for holiness, to Wesley, was the recognizable social fruits of love. And Wesley's life demonstrated his faith. He knew no holiness but a social holiness … Solitary religion is not to be found there. 'Holy Solitaries' is a phrase no more consistent with the Gospel than holy adulterers. The Gospel of Christ knows of no religion, but social; no holiness, but social holiness. Faith working by love is the length and breadth and depth and height of Christian perfection.[10]

Like the Pietists, Wesley and his followers engaged in a wide range of social ministries. In an age when lands were enclosed and people displaced to work in factories and coal mines, the evils of poverty, illiteracy, alcoholism, and disease were rife. Feeding the hungry, tending to the sick, visiting the prisoner, and showing strangers hospitality were common features of Methodism. Wesley provided lodging for widows, schooling for children, and short term loans for small businesses. Wesley also cared about health. Many persons lacked medical care, so he opened clinics, diagnosed illnesses, and prescribed cures.[11]

For Wesley, Christian life had a goal to produce maturing disciples who love God without reserve and who love neighbors in practical sacrificial Christ like ways. From these Spirit-infused dispositions comes the desire to love and serve the neighbor. This desire – in the logic of the divine economy – is a necessary (and utterly inevitable) concomitant to the desire for and love of God. Wesley states:

> The second great branch of Christian righteousness is closely and inseparably connected therewith, even 'Thou shalt love thy neighbor as thyself'. Thou Shalt Love – Thou shalt embrace with the most tender good will, the most earnest and cordial affection, the most inflamed desires of preventing or removing all evil, and of procuring for them every possible good. Thy Neighbor – That is not only thy friend, thy kinsman … not only the virtuous, the friendly, him that loves thee, that … returns thy kindness; but every human creature, every soul which God hath made; not excepting him whom thou knowest to be evil, and

[10] Wynkoop, *A Theology of Love*, p. 64.
[11] Knight III, 'John Wesley and the Quest for Holiness', p. 24.

unthankfully him that … persecutes thee: him shalt thou love as if thyself … [12]

Social Action

Thomas Fildes provides an illustration of a layman in the Methodist movement of the late 1700's devoted to this kind of practical social ministry from the Methodists. He was a founding member of the Strangers' Friends Society, which found the poorest of the poor and tended to them in Manchester England's burgeoning industrial tenement slums. From 1791 until the end of 1803, this society distributed what would have been roughly $14,000 to the poor in today's figures. Fildes was also instrumental in founding the first Sunday School for poor children in Manchester.[13] This is just one example of a man so moved by the work of God in his life and the sanctifying motivations to love God and others that he was mobilized to become involved and make a difference for others. This testimony could be multiplied many times during the Great Awakening of England and America and also in the Holiness Camp Meeting revivals of America.

Heritage of Love in Action

Consider the following snapshots from the heritage of Methodist and Holiness involvement with the poor.

Richard Allen, founder of the African Methodist Episcopal Church, was committed to the conviction of social equality for which Methodism stood for so long. He said that the Methodists were the first people that brought glad tidings to the 'colored people' of America. They transcended color and class, seeking salvation and pious living. He felt charity should be lifted and restored as a

---

[12] Stephen W. Rankin, 'The People Called Methodists', in Knight III (ed.), *From Aldersgate to Azusa Street*, pp 37, 40. See also Greathouse, *Love Made Perfect*, p. 52.

[13] Rankin, 'The People Called Methodists', p. 41. Remember that the origins of Sunday School ministry with Robert Rakes came from this same ethos, the desire to minister to children held captive in slums, poverty, and abuse in that age.

central tenant of the faith.[14] For this reason, restoring the central mission of charity to the Church, he began a denomination still known and influential today, the African Methodist Episcopal Church (AME).

Woven in the fiber of Phoebe Palmer's view of holiness was an inextricable message of human equality, which, quite frankly, changed the world for the disempowered of the 19th century in North America. She was thought to be a revivalist of the caliber and popularity of Charles Finney himself ... She started the famous Five Points Inner City Mission and is said to have produced a theological imperative that subsequently made women's charity work commonplace in America. For Palmer and many of these leaders, egalitarianism was not a side issue in the holiness movement that can easily be excised from its theology.[15]

The Free Methodists were against slavery and for ministry to the poor and, as their name suggests, standing against renting pews.[16] So we have yet one more denomination launched to safeguard the ideal of holistic mission! We cannot forget that Catherine and William Booth left the Methodist church to preach holiness and reach to the poor. They ultimately founded the Salvation Army out of their ministry in the East London Christian Mission.[17]

Phineas Bresee founded the Church of the Nazarene to minister in the neglected quarters of the cities through means of city missions, evangelistic services, house to house visitation, caring for the poor, and comfort for the dying.[18] John Alexander Dowie believed the implications of his Holiness message included social action with a welfare system, a home for orphans, a hospice for fallen women, a retirement home, and clear demonstration of equality of races.[19]

---

[14] Dennis C. Dickerson, 'Richard Allen and the Making of Early American Methodism', in Knight III (ed.), *From Aldersgate to Azusa Street*, pp. 73, 76.

[15] Diane K. Leclerc, 'Phoebe Palmer: Spreading Accessible Holiness', in Knight III (ed.), *From Aldersgate to Azusa Street:*, pp. 98, 93-94, 91.

[16] Douglas R. Cullum, 'Gospel Simplicity: Benjamin Titus Roberts and the Formation of the Free Methodist Church', in Knight III (ed.), *From Aldersgate to Azusa Street*, p. 102.

[17] Henry H. Knight III, 'The Later Nineteenth Century: Chastened Hope and Expectant Yearning', in Knight III (ed.), *From Aldersgate to Azusa Street*, p. 119.

[18] Harold E. Raser, 'Phineas Franklin Bresee: Recovering the Original Spirit of Methodism', in Knight III (ed.), *From Aldersgate to Azusa Street*, p. 175.

[19] D. William Faupel, 'John Alexander Dowie: Born to Command', in Knight III (ed.), *From Aldersgate to Azusa Street*, p. 183.

Aimee Simple McPherson of the Foursquare Church kept thousands from starving to death during the great depression.[20]

As I (RH) became aware of this significant heritage we have in holistic mission, I spoke to a ninety-two-year-old minister that has been involved in Holiness Pentecostal ministry for seventy years, traveling to over thirty nations, leading significant ministries for the Church of God of Prophecy, and under international leadership appointment for more than twenty-five years with that body. My questions were, 'Where did this emphasis on holistic mission go? When did it slip away?' The reason for my questions came from seeing the impressive history of holistic ministry recorded in our heritage and yet realizing that in my life time of involvement I was not aware of this history, nor had I seen such a central focus on holistic ministry promoted or demonstrated.

This seasoned minister felt that holistic ministries were diminished and lost through a variety of influences: 1) a shift to focus on an ecclesiology that suggested the lost would come to the people of God as their light shone ever brighter, 2) a sense that liberal churches took that ministry (the social gospel), deleting real salvation of the Gospel, therefore making it near to heresy for her holiness generation, or 3) the rise of government welfare seemed to justify the excuse of churches that people could get help now through government services.[21]

Terry Johns also makes the case that the theological shifts to individual decision for Christ in salvation also influenced the loss of social concern among Christian movements. Johns says,

> As the twentieth century unfolded, the focus on personal expressions of holiness began to overshadow the companion concern for social expressions ... The transition from personal commitment with corporate ethos continued to morph into a more individualistic understanding of salvation.

John mentions one reason for this transition as the adoption of the Evangelical emphasis on personal salvation, simplistically defined and narrowly focused, as forgiveness of sins in order to go to

[20]Kimberly Ervin Alexander, 'Restoration, Accommodation, and Innovation: The Contributions of Aimee Semple McPherson', in Knight III (ed.), *From Aldersgate to Azusa Street*, p. 254.

[21] Elva Howard, interviewed February 16, 2015 by Randy Howard.

heaven.[22] That shift saw an intensifying of the personal relationship with God while Wesley's associated concern for 'the neighbor' slipped away. The Wesleyan mantra of 'love for God and love for others' devolved to 'loving God'.

In hindsight it seems that the Wesleyan, Holiness, Pentecostal movements, and Christianity in general lost a huge strategy for glorifying God on the earth as the work of holistic mission slipped from prominence. In addition, Wesley's motivation was directly connected with his passion for holiness growing in the lives of his followers. He believed and led others to believe that loving and helping the brother was a 'means of grace' which would bear fruit in personal holiness.

For us today this may seem to be an amazing statement. Personal salvation, [particularly our life journey in sanctification and holiness] the Wesleys would argue, must be held together with social action in Christian discipleship.[23] It is true this is completely foreign to the way we view salvation today. But with this perspective as a fundamental of their faith these movements literally impacted their nations with compassionate holistic ministry as well as masses of lives transformed toward the image of Christ in 'holy love'.

Applications

Wesley not only felt 'works of piety' contributed grace to one's journey of sanctification, he firmly believed 'works of mercy' also contributed sanctifying grace. The Methodist movement was not all about sitting around and loving God in erudite ways; it was about God's love mobilizing believers to go and love others through acts of service and compassion. The recommended application for churches today would be to realize in mobilizing our people to acts of ministry and acts of mercy a church is facilitating their onward progress in grace toward holiness. A.J. Tomlinson seemed to understand this mobilization principle, using a favorite phrase, 'Every

---

[22] Terry Johns, 'The Practice of Holiness', in Knight III (ed.), *From Aldersgate to Azusa Street*, p. 302.
[23] Chilcote, *Recapturing the Wesleys' Vision*, p. 19.

member a worker and a work for every member'.[24] Many contemporary Pentecostals around the world seem to be recovering this original Wesleyan and Pentecostal emphasis; but, there is much more work to be done in this regard, especially in the United States.[25]

Wesley's genius was to connect the group activities of spiritual evaluation and support to the call to works of mercy. Therefore, the believers in the 'societies' and 'classes' (such as Thomas Fildes) also joined together to give offerings for the poor and to go out and help those in desperate need from their small communities. In so doing, they were enhancing their own spiritual development and growth toward 'holy love'. It is recommended that church leaders grasp this critical connection between spiritual development and acts of mercy so that the two are not divided in the philosophy of ministry at the local church. A church that grasps this should also help their people to understand that as we serve in compassion we are receiving grace that moves us closer to the image of Christ. As believers understand this they will feel an additional motivation to be involved and experience this infusion of grace. How often has it been said, 'We went to serve needy people, but we received greater blessings than we were able to give?' If the two are divided it will frustrate the call to service, making it an 'additional' and not an absolutely necessary function, diminishing motivation and blunting the sanctifying application.

Wesley felt all acts of mercy must also carry the gospel in some form. When mission and evangelism are separated there is no substantive connection between Christ and the cultural context into which the word is proclaimed. However, some believe the purpose of mission is only to make this world a better place. But Christian mission that flows from any source other than the good news of God's love in Jesus Christ is without substance and power. Wesley gave illustration of this synchronistic motion with evangelism and mission. There is an organic relationship between the two crucial Ministries, Evangelism and Mission. Evangelism is the heart;

---

[24] Lilly Dugger, *A. J. Tomlinson* (Cleveland, TN: White Wing Press, 1958).
[25] Donald E. Miller and Tetsunao Yamamori, *Global Pentecostalism: The New Face of Christian Social Engagement* (Berkley, CA: University of California Press, 2007).

mission is the body itself. The body moves in different contexts interacting and constantly at work. The dynamics of any setting determines how the body moves. But the heart is always beating. The heart is always sending blood out to all parts of the body. To separate the heart from the body is to kill it. Evangelism is the part of missions that motivates all the body to share the good news.[26] It is recommended that churches deny the trend today to do acts of mercy and abandon any expression of the gospel or God's saving purpose in life. Christian leaders today like to quote Saint Francis of Assisi, 'Preach the gospel ... and if necessary use words'. But Wesley linked mission and evangelism as inseparable. Wesley sent his followers out with great compassion and with gospel power (Rom. 1.16).

In this category of 'mobilization' we can include Wesley's practice of commissioning 'lay preachers'. This is certainly an advanced illustration of the lifting force at work among the Methodists. This practice was motivational, demonstrating that those who showed a sense of calling and accomplishment could find additional purpose and responsibility. It was also a means to multiply the leadership circle of the movement. The recommendation here could be that leaders will emerge from a track of spiritual development in sanctification. Since there are benefits from this for the Church body, preparation for this eventuality should be made.

John Wesley taught that the way to 'wait' for entire sanctification was to throw yourself into 'acts of piety' (prayer, worship, Communion, Christian conversation) and 'acts of mercy' (feeding the hungry, instructing the weak, clothing the naked, visiting the sick).[27] One of the points of this chapter is that Wesley promoted 'acts of mercy' among his people as a direct avenue to receive entire sanctification. We also see this in the opening quote from Saint Anthony, 'the person who does good to the neighbor, does good to the self'.[28] Somewhere through the years, this idea of serving the disadvantaged as a means of one's own sanctifying development has been lost. This *word from Wesley* would encourage us to reconnect acts of mercy to each person's spiritual quest for the image of Christ. If

---

[26] Chilcote, *Recapturing the Wesleys' Vision*, pp. 102-103.
[27] Greathouse, *Love Made Perfect*, p. 123.
[28] Bondi, *To Love as God Loves*, p. 28.

this be the case then this 'word' also would encourage churches to return to the field of serving the needy in force, since it is an avenue of discipleship as well as an act of mission. We know that mission and discipleship have been the two central mandates of the Church for centuries, and now Wesley helps remind us that they are both accomplished in great part through mobilizing ministry to the hurting and needy.

John Wesley's Prayer

O God, full of good and the One who does good, You extend Your loving acts to everyone in the world. Human beings are the works of Your hands, made in Your image and capable of knowing and loving You eternally. Help me to exclude none from my charity; all of us stand as objects of Your mercy. Let me treat my neighbors with that tender love which comes to Your children because You created them. You require love; it honors You.

Do not permit a single temptation to make my ungrateful or allow me to forfeit Your loving ways. Your kindness comes to us as better than Life itself! Grant that I assist all my brothers and sisters with prayers when I cannot reach them with actual services. Make me zealous to embrace all occasions for bringing people happiness by assisting the needy, protecting the oppressed, instructing the ignorant, confirming the wavering, exhorting the good, reproving the wicked. Amen.[29]

---

[29] Wesley, *Wesley's Daily Prayers*, p. 69.

6

PRESENTATION

By holiness I mean not fasting or bodily austerity or any other external means of improvement but that inward temper to which all these are subservient, a renewal of soul in the image of God. I mean a complex habit of lowliness, meekness, purity, faith, hope, and love of God and man.[1] – John Wesley

Wesley described grace in two parts, peace and power or favor and enabling. Justification dealt with our guilt and sin bringing peace, and sanctification gives us power, enabling us to refuse sin and it's dominion.[2]
— Kenneth J. Collins

Spiritual development involves both heart and head in holistic formation as the children of God. The Wesley's were firmly convinced that devotion apart from learning is rootless, and that knowledge devoid of piety is bankrupt. The uniting of heart and head in early Methodism was one of Wesley's most remarkable achievements. Essentially, the Christian life is a way of devotion.[3] – Paul Wesley Chilcote

In this final chapter, the aim is to push forward the conversation on how Christian leaders and ministries today can take the 'virtues' of the Wesleyan movement and apply them in our context of ministry. To begin, consider a brief summary of a few 'key virtues'.

---

[1] Collins, *John Wesley: A Theological Journey*, p. 52.
[2] Collins, *John Wesley: A Theological Journey*, p. 92.
[3] Chilcote, *Recapturing the Wesleys' Vision*, pp. 69-70.

Virtues of Wesleyan Strategies

In the low tide of spiritual fervor in Wesley's day, a response can be seen clearly in Wesley's life and ministry. He methodically (Methodists) went about the business of designing a new approach to ministry that carried the gospel effectively in a new environment, that targeted the most needy and massive segments of society, that introduced a structure to develop those that were drawn into this ministry, and that mobilized the majority of those attracted right back into service of some kind, all of which had a dramatic impact on the culture as a whole.

Possibly there are many who read this that would say, 'We need this same process at work today'. There might be many others that would say, 'How can we apply such concepts to our dilemma today?' Consider each component of that summary briefly:

Wesley designed a new approach to ministry in his day. Methodism obviously was something quite different than the Church of England was offering; so yes, it was new. At the same time, those who study Wesley see that he meticulously drew seeds from various sources out of Christian tradition to form his new approach. When the component parts are reviewed, nothing is really new except his inspiration to select, organize, and apply them so effectively.

Wesley proclaimed the gospel penetrating a new environment. For one, his gospel came with the ability (power) to transform lives. His movement holds this in common with so many genuine renewal movements of Christian history. Religion of Wesley's day had lost its grip on a gospel that could effectively make a difference. Second, Wesley's gospel immediately called people toward a long-range destiny in their Christian journey, the *telos* of holy love and being formed in the image of Christ.

Wesley targeted the most needy and massive segments of society. The words of Christ come to mind, 'They that are whole need not a physician, but they that are sick. I came not to call the righteous, but sinners to repentance' (Lk. 5.31-32). Wesley followed the model of Jesus, declaring a gospel of proven transformation to the poor and broken of society; and the result was spontaneous combustion. The most dynamic witness for the gospel is transformation, the blind man leaping and shouting 'I can see' (Jn 9.25), and the most receptive to this ministry are the oppressed and hurting.

Wesley introduced a structure to develop those that were drawn into this ministry. Because the *telos* of holy love was his ultimate goal, Wesley gave his greatest attention to moving his followers along the spiritual development continuum methodically (sanctification). This was his genius. His emphasis was on participation in the 'means of grace' through 'acts of piety' and 'acts of mercy' not as solitary believers but in forming groups he called 'societies, classes and bands'.

Wesley intended that this structure would mobilize the majority of those he attracted right back into service of some kind. The record is clear that the Methodists sent masses of Christian servants into the slums of England in the late 1700's and early 1800's to 'bind up the broken hearted and to proclaim liberty to the captives'. Wesley was convinced that with participation in mission, 'loving God by loving others', the lives of the servants were being formed by grace toward holy love, while the lives of those served were being drawn to the love of God through the tangible love they were experiencing.

Consider this direction for advancing a forum for dialogue: *Pentecostal Explorations for Holiness Today*. The question behind each 'Word from Wesley' has been, 'How can Christian leaders package this nugget and present it for effective ministry today?' In each chapter a segment has been devoted to making recommendations for application. Now in this 'Presentation' chapter the conversation presses ahead in hopes that it will go beyond this volume into forums of inspired or, perhaps, concerned Christian leaders on all levels, asking how can we use the innovations of Wesley that were so effective in his day to bring renewal generally, as well as renewal of the holiness/sanctification message and experience today?

This chapter will offer thoughts as conversation starters in a variety of directions and for various perspectives intended to facilitate the conversation for exploration in the renewal of the holiness/sanctification message in today's culture.

Central Elements to Consider

Jonathan Alvarado argues that Wesleyan theology is synergistic. 'It requires active cooperation from adherents and participation in the communal life of the Church through active participation'. He also says it is experiential, 'it tends toward a theology of encounter that would dramatically and drastically change people's lives'.[4] As a new holiness/sanctification presentation is considered, these two components will need to find their place of expression. How can people be led into synergistic participation with grace outlets that will change their lives and bring them into experiences of encounter, which activates transformation (2 Cor. 3.18)? This question is critical as applications for holiness/sanctification renewal are considered.

Wesley pointed people to the 'means of grace', which included 'acts of piety' and 'acts of mercy'. It was synergistic participation in these that was intended to activate the experiential, that is, encounters for transformation. Christian leaders must evaluate if these indeed continue to stand as means of grace? Are there others today that should be included? When these questions have been satisfied, we must press on to ask how will believers be led to active participation in the new and old means of grace that will be the key for life change?

Wesley felt strongly that there was no such thing as a solitary believer, and so he aimed to tap the power of believers joining together, helping one another work out their salvation, being formed as the Body of Christ. How can this be done most effectively in this culture? Wesley gave these groups penetrating questions to ask of one another.[5] Wesley established structures of accountability that

---

[4] Jonathan E. Alvarado, 'Twenty-First Century Holiness: Living at the Intersection of Wesleyan Theology and Contemporary Pentecostal Values', in Lee Roy Martin (ed.), *A Future for Holiness: Pentecostal Explorations* (Cleveland, TN: CPT Press, 2013), p. 243.

[5] An early list of Wesley's questions can be found online at https://home.snu. edu/~hculbert/selfexam.htm, accessed Feb. 1, 2017:

1. Am I consciously or unconsciously creating the impression that I am better than I really am? In other words, am I a hypocrite? 2. Do I confidentially pass on to others what has been said to me in confidence? 3. Can I be trusted? 4. Am I a slave to dress, friends, work or habits? 5. Am I self-conscious, self-pitying, or self-justifying? 6. Did the Bible live in me today? 7. Do I give the Bible time to speak to me every day? 8. Am I enjoying prayer? 9. When did I last speak to someone else of my faith? 10. Do I pray about the money I spend? 11. Do I get to bed on time and get up on time? 12. Do I disobey God in anything? 13. Do I insist upon doing something about which my conscience is uneasy? 14. Am I defeated in any part of my life? 15. Am I

provided leverage to keep believers on track. His groups were literally giving intensive pastoral care mobilized through laymen and women that would shepherd small groups of new and developing believers in the means of grace. It would seem necessary in order to crack the code for renewal in holiness and sanctification today that new structures for highly intentional small groups must be designed. It would be hard to deny that this was the critical vehicle that carried the momentum of Methodism to become a nation-changing influence in England in the late 1700's and early 1800's.

Finally, these conversations must include the path that new believers will be asked to journey toward the holiness/sanctification goal of holy love and the image of Christ. This would be a conversation about the *ordo salutis* – or more precisely in Wesleyan terms, the *via salutis* – the order of experiences a ministry intends believers to step through on their way to glorification. If it is all salvation, but there is no delineation, no road map, no path to follow in the footsteps of the Fathers toward holiness, then the mass of believers will tend to passivity and aimless meandering with no goal in sight. The mentality that God will lead them must be replaced, it seems, with the attitude that God will lead Christian leaders to lead them with purpose and structure toward a clear and biblical goal as he led John Wesley.

This would most likely include describing the goal (1) the steps along the way, (2) the vehicle to carry believers along, and (3) the activities (4) that nurture and form believers on the journey. In Wesley's ministry vision those components were (1) Christian perfection (goal), (2) Wesley's *ordo salutis* that included 'entire sanctification' (steps), (3) formation through societies, classes and bands with lay shepherds (vehicle), and (4) the means of grace found in acts of piety and acts of mercy (activities). One task for this conversation today and for Christian leaders is to discern what will these components become in our culture and for renewal of the holiness/sanctification message in our generation?

---

jealous, impure, critical, irritable, touchy or distrustful? 16. How do I spend my spare time? 17. Am I proud? 18. Do I thank God that I am not as other people, especially as the Pharisees who despised the publican? 19. Is there anyone whom I fear, dislike, disown, criticize, hold a resentment toward or disregard? If so, what am I doing about it? 20. Do I grumble or complain constantly? 21. Is Christ real to me?

The Elephant in the Room to Consider

With this framework of understanding we will now branch out to various implications that should be considered in a conversation about a contemporary 'presentation' of holiness/sanctification. Perhaps it is a good time to mention the 'elephant in the room' with regard to holiness/sanctification. Daniel Castelo touches on this as he discusses the difficulty in human agency and its relation to holiness. The 'impossibility of holiness' seems to be the trend of our day. Yet Castelo encourages believers by stating, 'No Christian could possibly argue that holiness is an impossibility in the Christian life, far too many authoritative materials suggest that the Trinity has made a species of holiness available to the Christian community here and now'.[6]

Of course, Castelo is speaking of actual moral theological holiness as opposed to simply 'positional' holiness, which attempts to give those who cannot embrace the real possibility of holiness today a theological footing on which to stand. This tension must be discussed and resolved if there is to be a widespread renewal in the holiness/sanctification message. Certainly, there are numerous reasons why different Christian groups have become hesitant if not resistant to promote or even talk about holiness/sanctification. No doubt 'works righteousness' has been one, where believers of past decades have fallen into the assumption that what they do will assist their salvation, giving a 'grace plus something' approach. This caution is real, and the Christian reaction is deep rooted. That strong fixation is interesting to note when observation and even current studies seem to indicate that license is a far greater threat today.

As the conversation ensues, Christian leaders will need wisdom to navigate the fears of the past while they try to deal with the problems of the present. Castelo reminds us, 'Holiness codes or prohibitions have created a distaste or aversion to material, bodily, and moral expressions of holiness because of their abuses. This might turn groups to positional understandings of holiness rather than moral theological understandings'.[7] Nevertheless, biblical witness

---

[6] Castelo, 'A Holy Reception Can Lead to a Holy Future', p. 228.
[7] Castelo, 'A Holy Reception Can Lead to a Holy Future', p. 228.

declares that believers can and should sanctify themselves. As believers, we are to purify and sanctify ourselves through covenant keeping practices of fidelity to God. Obedience and faithfulness are sanctifying and purifying features of the Christian life.

> A covenant framed life comes with obligations that are intrinsic to the quality, depth, and vitality of that life itself. 'Be holy' and 'be perfect' are not suggestions, but commands, yet with any command there is a veiled promise of God's faithfulness to help and enable us.[8]

If we look behind the former prohibitions, they attempted to create a workable sense of what is sacred and what is profane. The idea of concern over worldliness (in the sense of living by the standards of the present age rather than those of God's eternal kingdom) has all but disappeared today and should be a topic in these holiness conversations. Worldliness is not harmless fiction from a former age. It is a real threat to any believer's mind and soul, as well as to his life and body. Perhaps the former prohibitions were not the best strategy to secure some clarity and distinction between the world and God's realm, yet most Christian leaders have a sense that something must be in place identifying, or at least reminding, the Church of the 'threatening maleficent force' the world poses today.[9]

Perhaps most would agree that such a message has disappeared from our pulpits, churches, and Christian homes. The future of holiness depends on Christian leaders declaring the way forward holding the tension of decrying worldliness for the subtle but destructive evil that it wields and declaring the power of grace to save, deliver, protect, preserve, sanctify, and form believers into the image of Christ. As the Church learns from the past and receives guidance from the Spirit for the future the 'spirit' of the prohibitions can be embraced and applied without the 'substance' that so easily tended toward legalism. May Wesley's model encourage Christian leaders to roll up their sleeves to do the prayerful and arduous task of discerning God's way to proclaim the great hope of holiness and sanctification today.

---

[8] Castelo, 'A Holy Reception Can Lead to a Holy Future', p. 229.
[9] Castelo, 'A Holy Reception Can Lead to a Holy Future', p. 230.

Sanctification by The Spirit

To take a proactive stance as we shift from the prohibition challenge, the work of the Spirit must be considered in the work of sanctification and holiness.

> This I say then, walk in the Spirit and ye shall not fulfill the lust of the flesh (Gal. 5.16).

> God's love has been poured into our hearts through the Holy Spirit that has been given to us (Rom. 5.5 NRSV).

We see from these two scriptures clear biblical support for the work of the Holy Spirit in the sanctifying process, and naturally more can be identified. It was John Fletcher, a disciple of Wesley, and a keen Bible student, who described the work of the Spirit in this sanctification blessing even more than his mentor Wesley. For Fletcher, the Spirit was an active power working constantly to renew each individual. Additionally for him, the baptism in the Holy Spirit was 'entire sanctification'. He described the spiritual journey in the metaphors of Israel crossing the Red Sea leaving Egypt, parallel to justification and water baptism, and Israel crossing the Jordan River marching into Canaan, as parallel to Spirit baptism (entire sanctification for him). For Fletcher, Spirit baptism opened the way for entering the Promised Land of holiness of life, baptism in love, and Christian perfection.[10]

John Fletcher, Wesley's first interpreter, lifted the ministry of the Holy Spirit as a distinct agent of the work of sanctification. No doubt Paul encouraged his thoughts on this as Fletcher read 2 Thess. 2.13, 'sanctification by the Spirit' (NRSV); Rom. 15.16, 'sanctified by the Holy Spirit' (NRSV); and 1 Pet. 1.2, 'sanctified by the Spirit' (NRSV).

Prevenient grace was a large part of Wesley's theology to describe justification in terms different from the Reformed views of his day, and he was not hesitant to explain that it was the ministry of the Holy Spirit that was at work all through the earth drawing individuals and humanity toward God out of their fallen and depraved state. This is just one example where Fletcher's emphasis on

---

[10] Matthew K. Thompson, 'John Fletcher's Trinitarian Theology of Grace', in Knight III (ed.), *From Aldersgate to Azusa Street*, pp. 32-33.

the Spirit was in no way foreign to Wesley or his teachings. In fact, Leo George Cox spends considerable time listing theologians from Luther to Berkouwer that understood the Spirit as the agent of the sanctifying work.[11]

Dale Coulter expands on the presence and work of the Spirit in sanctification as he describes the empowering aspect of grace. It is the Spirit that transforms, elevates the soul, and draws the soul into fellowship with the Father through Christ. He mentions that Wesley particularly appreciated the synergistic cooperation of the Spirit with the individual in all the stages of the journey toward God. It is the Spirit that spreads the love of God through our hearts and activates the passions for God to such an extent that we can walk in the Spirit toward a new goal, holy love. By the Spirit, our desires are ordered rightly as love for God and love for the neighbor. Coulter says,

> We are empowered to move because the Spirit enters the person, initiating a movement that strengthens the will and opens the eyes of our heart to see God as the great lover of our soul. We find ourselves attracted to this God, an attraction that is not our own doing, but is the gift of God lest anyone should boast.[12]

J. Lyle Story explains, 'Love is the evidence of sanctification made experiential through the Holy Spirit'.[13] Story goes to Romans chapter eight to explain that holiness implies an ongoing relationship with God, as Christians are led by the Spirit (Rom. 8.14). Story notes that in this key chapter Paul unites the indicative of sanctification with the imperative, the declaration with the process. In chapter eight, the Spirit is mentioned 21 times in connection to the ethical implications for the believer (see verses 4, 5, 9, 13, 14, 16, 26, and cf. the fruit of the Spirit in Gal. 5.22). Story concludes by saying, 'The unfathomable love of Christ and the empowerment of the Spirit provide the incentive and the power for sanctification'.[14]

---

[11] Cox, *John Wesley's Concept of Perfection*, pp. 136-38.

[12] Coulter, 'A Wesleyan Understanding of Grace and Works'.

[13] J. Lyle Story, 'Pauline Thoughts about the Holy Spirit and Sanctification: Provision, Process, and Consummation', *Journal of Pentecostal Theology*, 18 (2009), p. 72.

[14] Story, 'Holy Spirit and Sanctification', pp. 81-82.

Bifurcation of the Spirit

With the birth and growth of the Pentecostal Movement there has been a regrettable bifurcation of the Spirit. It has been mentioned that John Fletcher thought of 'entire sanctification' as being the full baptism of the Spirit. Other groups could be listed in the development of the Holiness Movement that felt this at some level or other. The graphic title 'Fire Baptized', used by some in the history of the Holiness Movement, illustrates this idea of the central and essential work of the Spirit in sanctification for holiness.[15] Malachi 3 was one text giving support to the cleansing fire from God.

> Behold, I am going to send My messenger, and he will clear the way before Me. And the Lord, whom you seek, will suddenly come to his temple; and the messenger of the covenant, in whom you delight, behold, He is coming, says the Lord of hosts. [2] But who can endure the day of his coming? And who can stand when He appears? for He is like a refiner's fire and like fuller's soap. [3] He will sit as a smelter and purifier of silver, and He will purify the sons of Levi and refine them like gold and silver, so that they may present to the Lord offerings in righteousness. [4] Then the offering of Judah and Jerusalem will be pleasing to the Lord as in the days of old and as in former years (Mal. 3.1-4 (NASB).

The fire of the Spirit would burn away impurities and leave the pure refined ore of precious purity. After such a 'fire baptism' the gold ore would be so pure that the master founder could look down in the molten vat and see his own image. Songs of consecration followed such inspirations with phrases such as 'Oh burn away my feet of clay, and let me be consumed by Thy great fire, my one desire, no more of useless self, oh Lord, just more of Thee'.

---

[15] Consider the 'Fire Baptized Holiness Church of God' and later the 'Fire Baptized Holiness Church of God of the Americas'. These churches are more prominent than others in memory today, though 'Fire Baptized' was a graphic and emotive depiction of the work of the Spirit in sanctification for numerous holiness believers. http://fbhchurch.org/, accessed April 14, 2016. The Fire Baptized Holiness Church ultimately merged to form the vibrant denomination known today as the International Pentecostal Holiness Church.

As the Pentecostal Movement was born out of the Holiness Movement, the 'fire baptized' components for the most part transitioned into Pentecost along with others. The new experience then to be proclaimed, explained, and defended became the baptism of the Holy Spirit. Announcing this new experience effectively overshadowed the sanctifying ministry of the Spirit. Apologetics shifted in many camps to defining the Holy Spirit as different from the blessing of sanctification, as a means of fortifying validation for this additional Spirit blessing. The new and strong motivation to promote this freshly uncovered experience of Spirit baptism swept aside most efforts to describe sanctification as a work of the Spirit. In fact, this context made it somewhat conflictive. A clear division was needed between sanctification and the baptism in the Holy Spirit; therefore, bifurcation came about naturally as sanctification was described in its realm more and more as a work of grace; and the baptism of the Holy Spirit was described as the premier work of the Spirit. As this delineation arose, teaching about the role of the Spirit in sanctification gradually disappeared from everything but small pockets of the new Holiness Pentecostal Movement. In the development of the ministry of these authors, the idea of the Spirit playing a significant and even leading role in sanctification was only learned from historical study and not from the personal experiences of ministry from our beginning foundations. The line had been drawn decades earlier that sanctification was a work of grace that had little or nothing to do with the Holy Spirit.

The Spirit as Sanctifier

Perhaps today is the day to draw from the wells of Wesleyan history and John Fletcher's interpretations. As we discuss a new presentation for a believer's transforming journey in holiness and sanctification, could the leading role of the Holy Spirit provide us with substantial help? Among Pentecostal believers it is time to reopen the biblical wells of the work of the Spirit carrying us forward toward holy love.[16] And among all believers, the person of the Holy Spirit

---

[16] Of course, recovering the importance of holiness/sanctification as a premium work of the Holy Spirit does not entail relinquishing Classical Pentecostals' distinctive emphasis on charismatic endowment imparted through Spirit baptism.

has rarely been so freely discussed and embraced so widely. May the conversations on renewal in holiness fervor be greatly enhanced by the addition of this biblical agent of our sanctification, the sweet Holy Spirit.

Dale Coulter writes,

> If grace as power is the Spirit, who is the love of God poured out into the soul, then this love empowers us by igniting and inflaming our loves, that is, our emotions and desires. The power or strength of God is found in the way the Spirit rightly orders our emotions and desires toward God as our final end.[17]

Thus, perhaps it is not surprising that Coulter has earlier focused on the beauty of perfection and the desirability of holiness for Christian faith and life.[18] We heartily agree.

J. Lyle Story writes that Wesley was fascinated with a faith that could not only bring holiness, but also happiness. Surely that was missing from former generations of holiness seekers that were so desperately trapped in legalism and works righteousness. As the conversation grows about a new presentation for holiness this could be a contributing factor. Remember that genuine freedom is not freedom from guilt only (Rom. 5.1) but also freedom to love, a work of the Spirit (Rom. 5.5). In the Bible, the idea of purity is often connected to love and the promise of a new heart and a new spirit (Ezekiel 36). Story says, 'Love is the evidence of sanctification made experiential through the Holy Spirit'.[19]

Consecration and Postmodernism

In a conversation about the renewal of the holiness/sanctification message in today's culture consecration will demand a place. And as

---

[17] Coulter, 'A Wesleyan Understanding of Grace and Works'.

[18] Dale M. Coulter, *Holiness: The Beauty of Perfection* (Cleveland, TN: Pathway Press, 2004). A blurb from Cheryl Bridges Johns on the inside cover of this text indicates strong resonance with the present work:

> Dale Coulter's call to revisit the meaning of holiness is a timely message for today's church. It's a positive appeal that presents holiness as the joyful outcome of a restored relationship with God. For Coulter, holiness is not a dreary existence. It is a life of wonder and joyful fellowship with the triune God, who heals our brokenness and transforms us into the image of Christ.

[19] Story, 'Holy Spirit and Sanctification', pp. 71-72.

Christian leaders consider how this message can be packaged for a postmodern world, consecration holds critical challenges. Alvarado writes, 'When the basic framework of holiness is absent, churches tend to pursue pragmatic and functional utilitarianism, moral relativism, accommodations, and cultural tides'.[20] Obviously, these descriptors are at tension with consecration, surrender, and the life that sanctification offers in dying to oneself. Individualism, self actualization, consumerism, deconstruction, protest, and anti-establishment are words that are used to describe aspects of postmodernism.[21] The church that will rise to declare a renewed holiness/sanctification message has its work cut out for it. The words of Christ present a stark contrast, 'If any man will come after me, let him deny himself, and take up his cross daily, and follow me' (Lk. 9.23) Let the conversation begin!

Surely many contributions and inspirations will rise as this conversation forges ahead. One strong consideration for responding to these imposing realities of postmodernism is that long before the Church offers an institution, a dogma, or a hierarchy, the Church offers a person. Two significant descriptors used for the postmodern culture are 'relational' and 'experiential'. Christianity offers an invitation to a relationship with Christ, the Creator of all that is and Savior of mankind. Through the Living Word and the presence of the Holy Spirit, the spectrum of personal experience is without limit. The offer of the Bible is a relationship that promises experience day by day and moment by moment as Christ walks with believers today, exactly as he did in the pages of the New Testament.

An anchor point of faith for Wesley that must be applied in this consideration was his strong belief in 'spiritual encounter'. Wesley genuinely built his ministry based on his trust that if he could lead people to fountainheads of grace (means of grace), they would be changed and attracted to a life pursuit of God (holiness/sanctification). With all the challenges that postmodernism brings, Christian faith still holds the most powerful force mankind has ever known, the grace of God as administered by the work of the Holy Spirit

---

[20] Alvarado, 'Twenty-First Century Holiness', p. 239.
[21] See Kevin W. Mannoia and Don Thorsen (eds.), *The Holiness Manifesto* (Grand Rapids: Eerdmans, 2008). See also Millard J. Erickson, *Postmodernizing the Faith: Evangelical Responses to the Challenge of Postmodernism* (Grand Rapids, MI: Baker Books, 1998).

and presented in and through the person of Jesus Christ. Surely Christ as the cornerstone of Christian relating and experience is also the dynamic motivation for full Christian consecration and surrender, even in the face of postmodern challenges.[22]

Wesley wrote about the kind of impact 'spiritual encounter' made in Methodists in his tract, 'The Character of a Methodist':

> The love of God is shed abroad in his heart by the Holy Ghost, is happy in God, has hope of everlasting life, prays without ceasing, shows his love for God by loving his neighbors, seeks only to do God's will, manifests the fruit of the Spirit, keeps the commandments, never lives without accountability, does good to all men ...[23]

The Critical Question

Perhaps the most significant question to be tackled in these conversations that explore avenues for renewal of the holiness and sanctification message is, 'Can Christianity thrive without a vibrant holiness component?' Or, 'Can Christianity even survive without a significant holiness component?'

A brief scan of Christian history in any renewal source one might choose will quickly expose the fact that some resurgence of a call to moral theological holiness, that is, real and often radical life transformation, was fundamental to the renewal.[24] Go to the table of contents of those historical texts and read the headings. Nearly every chapter brings reflections of not only massive individual transformations but also of community transformations. Those texts validate that renewal moments in Christian history have been recorded consistently through the centuries and that the call to

---

[22] For more on Pentecostalism and the postmodernist mindset, see Jackie David Johns, 'Pentecostalism and the Postmodern Worldview', *Journal of Pentecostal Theology* 7 (1995), pp. 73-96, and Tony Richie, 'Becoming All Things, Spoiling the Egyptians, and Occupying Culture till Christ Comes: Reflections on the Recent Postmodernism Conversation', *The Pneuma Review* 12.1 (Winter 2009), pp. 31-47.

[23] John Wesley, 'The Character of a Methodist', in *The Works of John Wesley* (ed. Jackson), VIII, pp. 340-47. See Chapter 3 for a fuller rendering of this description.

[24] Consider Wesley Duewel's work, *Revival Fire* (Grand Rapids, MI: Zondervan Publishing House, 1995).

moral theological holiness of life was woven through the majority of them. It is almost as if history, guided by the hand of God, is testifying to the fact that the Church of our Lord Jesus Christ can neither thrive nor survive without a fresh call into the presence of our Holy God and a fresh touch of his consuming fire to purify.[25]

The authors can remember the 'church growth' era of the seventies, then later the 'church health' era and beyond. The age of technology was flourishing and the Church was experiencing the thrill of implementing such new ideas to ministry. Most would agree that help in making the work of the Church more professional, efficient, and excellent was desperately needed as all of commerce and industry surged in those areas. In the five decades from the seventies there have been numerous new and innovative influences adapted to keep the Church abreast with the times somewhat. Nevertheless, in those five decades the Christian church of America has grossly undergrown compared to the population growth.[26]

This volume asks the question if perhaps a different kind of innovation is needed additionally, innovation similar in concept to the innovations in ministry that John Wesley led in his own age? It is obvious that those innovations from Wesley gave a central focus to the call to holiness, which seems to have disappeared in these five decades. Could there be a connection between the decline of these five decades and the quality of biblical Christianity produced in churches where little holiness message can be found? Whatever the factual answer, this is surely a critical question in the conversation espoused here.

In these most recent five decades a grand sweeping shift has taken place in world Christianity. This has been chronicled by missiologists such as David Barrett, of *The World Christian Encyclopedia*,

---

[25] Indeed, arguably the Church uniquely and authentically exists only as (and/or in) 'sanctified community'. See Matthias Wenk, 'The Church as Sanctified Community', in John Christopher Thomas (ed.), *Toward a Pentecostal Ecclesiology: The Church and the Fivefold Gospel* (Cleveland, TN: CPT, 2010), pp. 105-38.

[26] Kelly Shattuck, 'Seven Startling Facts: An Up Close Look At Church Attendance in America', online http://www.churchleaders.com/pastors/pastor-articles/139575-7-startling-facts-an-up-close-look-at-church-attendance-in-america.html/5, *Church Leaders*, accessed June 15, 2016.

or Philip Jenkins, in his book *The Next Christendom*, or Harvard Professor, Harvey Cox, in his work, *Fire from Heaven*, to name a few.[27] While the western world of Christianity has experienced difficult times since the decade of the seventies it seems the remainder of the Christian world has experienced an amazing phenomenon which is described in these works and many more. One study by the Pew Forum on Religion and Public Life entitled 'Spirit and Power: A 10 Country Survey of Pentecostals' describes from analytical surveys the behaviors of people that have experienced life transformation in this season of renewal.[28] Yamamori and Miller share the findings of a five-year global study in their volume, *Global Pentecostalism*, where renewal has energized amazing innovations in life and community transformation.[29] George Otis Jr. has spent years researching locations where genuine community transformation has been verified to bring to the world the testimony of the gracious acts of God for this day.[30] Such reports give hope to the western world that renewal on a wide scale similar to the age of John Wesley in England is possible today.

So, we return to our primary questions for this critical conversation. 'Can Christianity thrive without a vibrant holiness component?' Or, 'Can Christianity even survive without a significant holiness component?' Many would suggest that Christianity in the west over the last five decades is an example of Christian faith that has not been able to thrive and is struggling to survive when the call to

---

[27] See Philip Jenkins, *The Next Christendom: The Coming of Global Christianity* (New York, NY: Oxford University Press, 2002), David Barrett's annual research updates published in the 'International Bulletin of Missionary Research' each January; Harvey Cox, *Fire From Heaven: The Rise of Pentecostal Spirituality and the Reshaping of Religion in the Twenty-First Century* (Reading, MA: Addison-Wesley Publishing Company, 1995); Vinson Synan, *An Eyewitness Remembers the Century of the Holy Spirit* (Grand Rapids, MI: Chosen of Baker Books, 2010); Jack Hayford, *The Charismatic Century: The Enduring Impact of the Azusa Street Revival* (New York, NY: Warner Faith Books, 2006); Bryant L. Myers, *The New Context of World Mission* (Monrovia, CA: Missions Advanced Research Communications Center, 1996) as sources describing the growth and influence of the Pentecostal movement globally, especially in its vibrant life and leadership.

[28] Pew Forum on Religion and Public Life, 'Spirit and Power: A 10 Country Survey of Pentecostals' (Washington DC: Pew Research Center, 2006).

[29] Miller and Yamamori, *Global Pentecostalism*.

[30] George Otis Jr., *Transformations I and Transformations II* (Colorado Springs: Sentinel Group, 1996).

holiness has been diminished. The biblical record affirms that holiness is critical to the life and health of Christianity. The historical record also stands as a witness. And today the contemporary world Christian movement demonstrates the vibrant life that a genuine moral theological call to holiness can bring.

For those that are convinced this is the case, that the holiness/sanctification message must have a significant place in Christianity, let us begin to gather around coffee tables and prayer cells. Let us begin to dream the dream of inspiration as Wesley before us, the dream of how a generation can be renewed in the love of God so thoroughly that it will be reflected in massive life transformations and therefore community-wide transformations. Let us pour out our hearts and hopes that Christ's Body can be transformed by grace, purified by his blood, and formed into his image. And then let us roll up our sleeves and get down to the business of designing, by heaven's inspirations, ministry structures and patterns that will have relevance and attraction to our western culture today. Let John Wesley encourage us with words from the inspiration and success of his day and his nation shaking ministry. By God's grace a new Awakening can begin!

John Wesley's Prayer

We ask You to hear us, dear Lord, that You illuminate all ministers of Your Gospel with true knowledge and understanding of Your Word, so that both by their preaching and living they will speak and show its truth. Amen.[31]

Strengthen the hearts of us Your servants against all corruptions and temptations. Enable us to give ourselves faithfully and entirely to Your service.

Grant us the gift of encouraging each other to love and serve You, and for maturing respect and love for You so we can help You build Your heavenly kingdom.

More, by your infinite mercies, help us to bring ourselves at last to You to live with those who have died in Christ. Then may we rejoice together before You through the merits of

---

[31] Wesley, *Wesley's Daily Prayers*, p. 379.

our Lord, Jesus Christ, to Whom with You and the Holy
Spirit, the blessed and only Potentate, the King of kings and
Lord of lords, to Whom we acknowledge honor and power
eternally. Amen.[32]

---

[32] Wesley, *Wesley's Daily Prayers*, p. 391.

BIBLIOGRAPHY

Adewuya, J. Ayodeji, *Holiness in the Letters of Paul: The Necessary Response to the Gospel* (Eugene, OR: Cascade, 2016).

Alexander, Kimberly Ervin, 'Restoration, Accommodation, and Innovation: The Contributions of Aimee Semple McPherson', in Henry H. Knight III (ed.), *From Aldersgate to Azusa Street: Wesleyan, Holiness, and Pentecostal Visions of the New Creation* (Eugene, OR: Pickwick Publications, 2010), pp. 246-55.

Alvarado, Jonathan E., 'Twenty-First Century Holiness: Living at the Intersection of Wesleyan Theology and Contemporary Pentecostal Values', in Lee Roy Martin (ed.), *A Future for Holiness: Pentecostal Explorations* (Cleveland, TN: CPT Press, 2013), pp. 237-51.

Anderson, Robert Mapes, *Vision of the Disinherited: The Making of American Pentecostalism* (Oxford: Oxford University Press), 1979.

Arnold, Clinton E. 'Early Church Catechesis and New Christians' Classes in Contemporary Evangelicalism' *Journal of the Evangelical Theological Society* 47.1 (March 2004), pp. 39-54.

Baker, John and Rick Warren, *Celebrate Recovery* (Saddleback, CA: Saddleback Resources, 2007).

Balmer, Randall, *Religion in American Life: A Short History* (Oxford/New York: Oxford University Press, 2008).

Barna Group, 'The Concept of Holiness Baffles Most Christians'. Online article cited May 15, 2015. https://www.barna.org/barna-update/5-barna-update/162-the-concept-of-holiness-baffles-most-americans#.VS1g3_nF-ik.

Blackaby, Henry and Claude King, *Experiencing God* (Nashville: B&H Publishing, 2008).

Bondi, Roberta C., *To Love as God Loves* (Philadelphia, PA: Fortress Press, 1984).

Castelo, Daniel, 'A Holy Reception Can Lead to a Holy Future', in Lee Roy Martin (ed.), *A Future for Holiness: Pentecostal Explorations* (Cleveland, TN: CPT Press, 2013), pp. 225-36.

Chan, Francis, *Crazy Love* (Colorado Springs: David C. Cook, 2008).

Chilcote, Paul Wesley, *Recapturing the Wesleys' Vision: An Introduction to the Faith of John and Charles Wesley* (Downers Grove, IL: IVP Academic, 2003).

'Clement of Alexandria: Theologian of the Intelligentsia', *Christianity Today* (March 23, 2016 from http://www.christianitytoday.com/ history/people/evangelistsandapologists/clement-of-alexandria. html.

Coulter, Dale M., *Holiness: The Beauty of Perfection* (Cleveland, TN: Pathway Press, 2004).

—'A Wesleyan Understanding of Grace and Works', Cited online May 15, 2015, The Seedbed Blog. http://seedbed.com/feed/ wes leyan-understanding-grace-works/.

Cox, Harvey, *Fire from Heaven: The Rise of Pentecostal Spirituality and the Reshaping of Religion in the Twenty-First Century* (Reading, MA: Addison-Wesley Publishing Company, 1995).

Cox, Leo George, *John Wesley's Concept of Perfection* (Nicholasville, KY: Schmul Publishing, 1999).

Crosby, Robert C., 'Joshua's Holy Ground Experience', in Lee Roy Martin (ed.), *A Future for Holiness: Pentecostal Explorations* (Cleveland, TN: CPT Press, 2013), pp. 24-47.

Cullum, Douglas R., 'Gospel Simplicity: Benjamin Titus Roberts and the Formation of the Free Methodist Church', in Henry H. Knight III (ed.), *From Aldersgate to Azusa Street: Wesleyan, Holiness, and Pentecostal Visions of the New Creation* (Eugene, OR: Pickwick Publications, 2010), pp. 99-108.

Dayton, William T., 'Entire Sanctification: The Divine Purification and Perfection of Man', in C.W. Carter and R.D. Thompson, and C.R. Wilson (eds.), *A Contemporary Wesleyan Theology: Biblical, Systematic, and Practical* (Grand Rapids: Zondervan, 1983), I, pp. 521-65.

Dickerson, Dennis C. 'Richard Allen and the Making of Early American Methodism', in Henry H. Knight III (ed.), *From Aldersgate to Azusa Street: Wesleyan, Holiness, and Pentecostal Visions of the New Creation* (Eugene, OR: Pickwick Publications, 2010), pp. 72-77.

Drury, John L. 'Barth and Testimony', in C.T. Collins Winn and J.L. Drury, *Karl Barth and the Future of Evangelical Theology* (Eugene, OR: Wipf and Stock Pub., 2014), pp. 102-14.

Drury, Keith. 'The Holiness Movement is Dead', *Counterpoint Dialogue* online cited May 15, 2015, http://www.fwponline.cc/v24i1/review%20two.html.

Duewel, Wesley, *Revival Fire* (Grand Rapids, MI: Zondervan Publishing House, 1995).

Dugger, Lilly, *A.J. Tomlinson* (Cleveland, TN: White Wing Press, 1958).

Dyck, Drew, *Yawning at Tigers: You Can't Tame God So Stop Trying* (Nashville: Nelson Publishers, 2014).

Ellington, Scott, 'Have We Been Sanctified?: Renewing the Role of Experience in Interpreting Biblical Texts', in Lee Roy Martin (ed.), *A Future for Holiness: Pentecostal Explorations* (Cleveland, TN: CPT Press, 2013), pp. 107-26.

Erickson, Millard J., *Postmodernizing the Faith: Evangelical Responses to the Challenge of Postmodernism* (Grand Rapids, MI: Baker Books, 1998).

Faupel, D. William, 'John Alexander Dowie: Born to Command', in Henry H. Knight III (ed.), *From Aldersgate to Azusa Street: Wesleyan, Holiness, and Pentecostal Visions of the New Creation* (Eugene, OR: Pickwick Publications, 2010), pp. 177-84.

Gause, Hollis, *Living in the Spirit: The Way of Salvation*, (Cleveland, TN: Pathway Press, 1980).

Greathouse, William, *Love Made Perfect: Foundations for the Holy Life* (Kansas City, MO: Beacon Hill, 1997).

Green, Chris, *Sanctifying Interpretation: Vocation, Holiness and Scripture* (Cleveland, TN: CPT Press, 2015).

Harper, Steve, *The Way to Heaven: The Gospel According to John Wesley* (Grand Rapids: Zondervan, 2003).

Hayford, Jack, *The Charismatic Century: The Enduring Impact of the Azusa Street Revival* (New York, NY: Warner Faith Books, 2006).

Hill, A.M. *Holiness and Power for the Church and the Ministry* (New York: Garland Publishing, 1984).

Howard, Elva, Interviewed February 16, 2015 by Randy Howard in Cleveland, TN.

Jenkins, Philip, *The Next Christendom: The Coming of Global Christianity* (New York, NY: Oxford University Press, 2002.

Johns, Cheryl Bridges, *Pentecostal Formation: A Pedagogy Among the Oppressed* (JPTSup 2; Sheffield, UK: Sheffield Academic Press, 1993).

Johns, Jackie David, 'Pentecostalism and the Postmodern Worldview', *Journal of Pentecostal Theology* 7 (1995), pp. 73-96.

Johns, Terry, 'The Practice of Holiness: Implications for a Pentecostal Moral Theology', in Lee Roy Martin (ed.), *A Future for Holiness: Pentecostal Explorations* (Cleveland, TN: CPT Press, 2013), pp. 297-311.

Knight III, Henry H. 'The Eighteenth Century: The Birth of Methodism', in Henry H. Knight III (ed.), *From Aldersgate to Azusa Street: Wesleyan, Holiness, and Pentecostal Visions of the New Creation* (Eugene, OR: Pickwick Publications, 2010), pp. 13-16.

—'John Wesley and the Quest for Holiness', in Henry H. Knight III (ed.), *From Aldersgate to Azusa Street: Wesleyan, Holiness, and Pentecostal Visions of the New Creation* (Eugene, OR: Pickwick Publications, 2010), pp. 17-26.

—The Later Nineteenth Century: Chastened Hope and Expectant Yearning', in Henry H. Knight III (ed.), *From Aldersgate to Azusa Street: Wesleyan, Holiness, and Pentecostal Visions of the New Creation* (Eugene, OR: Pickwick Publications, 2010), pp. 115-24.

LaCugna, Catherine Mowery, *God for Us: The Trinity and Christian Life* (San Francisco: Harper, 1991).

Land, Steven Jack, *Pentecostal Spirituality: A Passion for the Kingdom* (Cleveland, TN: CPT Press, 2010).

Leclerc, Diane K., 'Phoebe Palmer: Spreading Accessible Holiness', in Henry H. Knight III (ed.), *From Aldersgate to Azusa Street: Wesleyan, Holiness, and Pentecostal Visions of the New Creation* (Eugene, OR: Pickwick Publications, 2010), pp. 90-98.

Mannoia, Kevin W. and Don Thorsen (eds.), *The Holiness Manifesto* (Grand Rapids: Eerdmans, 2008).

Marshall, I. Howard, *1 Peter* (IVPNTC; Downers Grove: Intervarsity Press, 1991).

Martin, Lee Roy, *Fasting: A Centre for Pentecostal Theology Short Introduction* (Cleveland, TN: CPT Press, 2014).

McCracken, Brett, 'Have Christians Lost Their Sense of Difference?' Online cited May 15, 2015 on Mere Orthodoxy blog: http://mere orthodoxy.com/have-christians-lost-their-sense-of-difference/.

Miller, Donald E. and Tetsunao Yamamori, *Global Pentecostalism: The New Face of Christian Social Engagement* (Berkley, CA: University of California Press, 2007).

Moltmann, Jürgen, *The Trinity and the Kingdom of God* (Minneapolis: Fortress Press, 1993).

Myers, Bryant L., *The New Context of World Mission* (Monrovia, CA: Missions Advanced Research Communications Center, 1996).

Oden, Thomas C., *Wesley's Scriptural Christianity: A Plain Exposition of His Teaching on Christian Doctrine* (Grand Rapids, MI: Zondervan Publishing, 1994).

Otis Jr., George, *Transformations I and Transformations II* (Colorado Springs: Sentinel Group. 1996).

Outler, Albert C., *John Wesley* (New York: Oxford, 1964, 1980).

Peterson, David, *Possessed by God: A New Testament Theology of Sanctification and Holiness* (Grand Rapids, MI: Eerdmans, 1995).

Pew Forum on Religion and Public Life, 'Spirit and Power: A 10 Country Survey of Pentecostals' (Washington DC: Pew Research Center, 2006).

Rainy, Russ, 'Summary of the Willow Creek Study' The Christian Coaching Center. Cited Jan. 2, 2016. http://www.christiancoachingcenter.org/index.php/russ-rainey/coachingchurch2/.

Rankin, Stephen W., 'The People Called Methodists', in Henry H. Knight III (ed.), *From Aldersgate to Azusa Street: Wesleyan, Holiness, and Pentecostal Visions of the New Creation* (Eugene, OR: Pickwick Publications, 2010), pp. 36-44.

Raser, Harold E., 'Phineas Franklin Bresee: Recovering the Original Spirit of Methodism', in Henry H. Knight III (ed.), *From Aldersgate to Azusa Street: Wesleyan, Holiness, and Pentecostal Visions of the New Creation* (Eugene, OR: Pickwick Publications, 2010), pp. 167-77.

Richie, Tony, 'Becoming All Things, Spoiling the Egyptians, and Occupying Culture till Christ Comes: Reflections on the Recent Postmodernism Conversation', *The Pneuma Review* 12.1 (Winter 2009), pp. 31-47.

—'Spiritual Transformation through Pentecostal Testimony', David S.E. Han and Jackie David Johns (eds.), *Knowing God in the Ordinary Practices of the Christian Life* (Cleveland, TN: CPT Press, forthcoming).

Runyon, Theodore, *The New Creation: John Wesley's Theology Today* (Nashville: Abingdon Press, 1998).

Shattuck, Kelly, 'Seven Startling Facts: An Up Close Look At Church Attendance in America'. Cited online June 15, 2016 in Church Leaders: http://www.churchleaders.com/pastors/pastor-articles /139575-7-startling-facts-an-up-close-look-at-church-attendance - in-america.html/5.

Smith, Brandon B., 'John Wesley's Christian Perfection: Myths, Realities, and Critique'. Cited online May 15, 2015 in Patheos Conversations on Faith: <http://www.patheos.com/blogs/brandond smith/2015/03/john-wesleys-christian-perfection-myths-realities-and-critique/#ixzz3XrXKaxdK>.

Smith, James K.A., *Desiring the Kingdom* (Grand Rapids, MI: Baker Academics, 2009).

Story, J. Lyle, 'Pauline Thoughts about the Holy Spirit and Sanctification: Provision, Process, and Consummation', *Journal of Pentecostal Theology* 18 (2009), pp. 67-94.

Synan, Vinson, *An Eyewitness Remembers the Century of the Holy Spirit* (Grand Rapids, MI: Chosen Books, 2010).

Tenney, Tommy, *God Chasers* (Shippensburg, PA: Destiny Image, 1998).

Thayer, Joseph, *Thayer's Greek-English Lexicon of the New Testament* (New York: Hendrickson Publishers, 1996).

Thompson, Matthew K., 'John Fletcher's Trinitarian Theology of Grace', in Henry H. Knight III (ed.), *From Aldersgate to Azusa Street: Wesleyan, Holiness, and Pentecostal Visions of the New Creation* (Eugene, OR: Pickwick Publications, 2010), pp. 33-55.

Thorsen, Don, *The Wesleyan Quadrilateral: Scripture, Tradition, Reason, and Experience as a Model of Evangelical Theology* (Lexington, KY: Emeth Press, 2005 edition [originally 1990]).

Vest, R. Lamar and Steven Land, *Reclaiming Your Testimony: Your Story and the Christian Story* (Cleveland, TN: Pathway Press, 2002).

Volf, Miroslav, *After Our Likeness: The Church as the Image of the Trinity* (Grand Rapids, Eerdmans, 1998).

Wallis, Jim, 'Can You Really Tell A Difference?' Online citation May 15, 2015: http://sojo.net/blogs/2013/09/26/can-you-really-tell-difference-between-christians-and-non-christians.

Warren, Rick, *The Purpose Driven Life* (Grand Rapids: Zondervan, 2002).

Wenk, Matthias, 'The Church as Sanctified Community', in John Christopher Thomas (ed.), *Toward a Pentecostal Ecclesiology: The Church and the Fivefold Gospel* (Cleveland, TN: CPT, 2010), pp. 105-38.

Wesley, John, *A Plain Account of Christian Perfection* (Peabody, MA: Hendrickson, 2007).

—*The Letters of John Wesley* (ed. John Telford; London: Epworth, 1931).

—*The Life of John Wesley* (ed. John Telford; New York: Eaton and Mains, 1929).

—*The Works of John Wesley* (ed. Rupert E. Davies; Nashville: Abingdon Press, Bicentennial edn, 1989).

—*The Works of John Wesley* (ed. Thomas Jackson; Grand Rapids, MI: Baker Books, 1979).

—*The Works of the Rev. John Wesley* (London: Wesleyan Methodist Book Room, 3rd edn, 1872).

—*Wesley's Daily Prayers: Prayers for Every Day in the Year* (ed. Donald E. Demaray; Anderson, IN: Bristol House, 1998).

Wynkoop, Mildred Bangs, *A Theology of Love: The Dynamic of Wesleyanism* (Kansas City, MO: Beacon Hill, 1972).

Ziefle, Joshua, 'From Fear-Based to Holiness-Based: Thoughts About the Work of the Holy Spirit in Youth Ministry', in Lee Roy Martin (ed.), *A Future for Holiness: Pentecostal Explorations* (Cleveland, TN: CPT Press, 2013), pp. 333-47.

Index of Biblical (and Other Ancient) References

Index of Names

53, 59, 65, 66, 69, 72, 73, 74, 81, 86,
    88, 89, 96, 97, 99, 103, 112, 113,
    114, 115
Whitfield (Whitefield), G.   16, 62, 63,
    80
Willard, D.   82

Wynkoop, M.B.   31, 32, 33, 34, 35, 36,
    40, 41, 43, 75, 89, 90
Yamamori, T.   95, 114
Ziefle, J.   44
Zinzendorf, N.   16

Made in the USA
Columbia, SC
18 May 2024